BODH

ITS SIGNIFICANCE IN THE 21ST CENTURY

NISSOKA

indhorse Publications

Published by
Windhorse Publications
169 Mill Road
Cambridge
CB1 3AN
United Kingdom

info@windhorsepublications.com
www.windhorsepublications.com

All profits from sales of this book will go to developing
the Three Jewels Centre at Bodh Gaya.

ISBN: 978-1-909314-07-8

Contents

Foreword

Bodh Gaya is a place that has touched me deeply. For a few years, up until the year 2000, I went out to India in December and taught meditation and Buddhism on the roof of the Maha Bodhi Society. I was invited as guest teacher by Lalitavajra, an early pioneer of the Triratna Order in India. Nissoka, who was then Julian Bennett, used to help set up the classes. The monks at the Maha Bodhi Society knew my teacher Sangharakshita as an esteemed former editor of their magazine, the Maha Bodhi Journal, and were very keen that his disciples, ordained members of the Triratna Order, should teach there. They were especially concerned that western pilgrims received teaching appropriate for their needs and outlook, and they knew that Sangharakshita's approach worked in the west. Lalitavajra, Julian and I enjoyed our hours on their roof, teaching meditation in the morning and evening to appreciative young westerners, mostly on the hippy trail. It also felt an honour that we had been asked to teach by the successors of the saintly Anagarika Dharmapala, who in the Victorian era made the first Buddhist connection for centuries with the actual site of the Buddha's Enlightenment and whose activism made possible the entire modern Buddhist presence in Bodh Gaya. But what I remember best is the feeling of waking up in the rosy light of the north Indian dawn and going down to the bodhi tree each day to give myself up for hours to meditation in the company of silent yogis and prostrating monks.

At times we would visit local monasteries and converse, sometimes at length, with a head monk. Some of these conversations were profoundly inspiring and I began to realise the unique character of Bodh Gaya, where Buddhist traditions were all sharing what they had in common. These mostly elderly, experienced monks had been well chosen for their special, almost diplomatic task. The ones I met had studied and meditated deeply and were filled with humility and wisdom, concerned to communicate well. All shared a deep appreciation – an appreciation that came from experience – of what the Buddha had done in discovering Enlightenment.

It was exciting to realise that this place was making a unique contribution to connecting together all the disparate communities of Dhamma practitioners, stretching from Afghanistan to Japan. The barriers between different groups of Buddhists had been beginning to dissolve in the literary world, and it was also starting to happen via the early Internet. But these are intangible, abstract worlds. Here in this extraordinary place Buddhist traditions were coming together for the first time in a physical and personal way, as people actually lived and practised together. Nowhere else in the world could have drawn together so many different traditions of Buddhism, for this is where it had all started. In those days I recall there being twenty or so temples. Nowadays of course there are many more, and there are hotels and huge Buddha images and many more tourists and pilgrims, and yet more latter day Dhamma practitioners coming together to celebrate their great inheritance. I am so glad to know that Nissoka has carried on all these years and has helped develop our own centre in Bodh Gaya. Nowadays the Triratna Order worldwide comes together here for retreats, and hundreds of Indian-born Order members meditate along with visitors from the USA, Europe and many countries.

My last visit was memorable. It was the millennium, the point at which (at least according to the calendar of the western world) we moved into the 21st century. We did a ceremony to mark the occasion on Triratna's land at Bodh Gaya along with a number of people attending the Maha Bodhi Society teachings. I knew that from this point, our presence here in Bodh Gaya was going to grow. An important transition was being made.

Since then I've not been back to Bodh Gaya, but now the Three Jewels Centre has been established there, and this important book marks a further transition. May what happened at the bodhi tree continue to inspire pilgrims and all who aspire to Enlightenment worldwide.

Kamalashila

Introduction

This book is the fruit of a labour of love, written by a man who is deeply inspired by his subject. Nissoka has given his life to Bodh Gaya in a manner that reminds one of an age perhaps now past, when pilgrims would prostrate all the way from Lhasa to the foot of the bodhi tree, or spend their entire savings to buy gold leaf with which to gild the Buddha's image. For Nissoka, the mighty Tree of Enlightenment, together with the temple in which it is located, has become the complete focus of his Dhamma practice, even of his life. For him, it contains uncountable riches and infinite meaning. It is an array of these riches and a hint of this meaning that he has laid out for us here in his own unvarnished and passionate style. This in itself is a great gift. The best gift he brings us in his book, however, is himself: a man who has faced his own decay and made of himself an offering to what for all Buddhists must be the most significant place in this world, into which is distilled the entire meaning of our existence.

Dhammachari Subhuti

Author's preface

I have had a deep connection with Bodh Gaya, the place where the Buddha gained Enlightenment more than 2,500 years ago, ever since my first visit there in 1998. In the years since then I have helped to set up a Dhamma centre there, under the inspiration of my teacher, Sangharakshita, and the Buddhist movement he founded, the Triratna (Three Jewels) Buddhist Order.

I became a Buddhist in 1994 and was ordained into the Triratna order in 2001. I have lived in Bodh Gaya each winter since 1998, running Dhamma classes with Lalitavajra, Lokabandhu, Kamalashila and Adarsha, and then helping to develop our centre there in its early years. I endure a marathon of pain every time I go to India because of an accident I sustained in 1990 when serving in the Parachute Regiment. I injured my back in a vehicle accident whilst working in Botswana, and have been in immense pain every day since then. So most of this book has been written lying down.

I also have Huntington's disease, a terminal illness which will mean my functioning will begin to fail and my actions will become uncontrollable until I die from the disease. It usually takes ten to fifteen years for a person with Huntington's to die once illness starts. I have already started to experience some of the early symptoms. It is hereditary; I have lost three members of my close family to it and more will die, including me. Although I have a terminal illness, I am fully committed to serving the Buddha at Bodh Gaya until I physically can't any more. I want my final years to be spent giving all I can to serving here, so that when my body and mind fall apart I will have an unbreakable connection with this place.

Directly serving the Buddha, I spend hours sitting at the bodhi tree soaking up the Buddha's influence. I ask him: 'What do you want me to do now? I am your flesh and your voice; what do you want from me?' I am committed to serving him for life. I feel so blessed to have daily direct contact with the peace emanating from the spot where his liberation took place.

In this book I want to offer some of my reflections about Bodh Gaya and our movement's relationship with this most sacred place. If you have never been to Bodh Gaya, I hope I can give you a glimpse of its significance and inspire you to come here. If you have been before, I hope I can stir fond memories, and if you cannot come here, I hope I can spark your imagination and lift your heart, so that you too feel that you have made this pilgrimage.

I have written the book for all Dhamma practitioners, but especially for my fellow members of the Triratna community. I find it very hard to express the profound feelings and thoughts that have arisen in me while I have lived in Bodh Gaya, and it is impossible to do the place justice in words, but I hope I can give you at least a sense of it – enough to make you want to make the journey yourself. Bodh Gaya is in constant evolution, a dynamic energy that is forever changing and growing, and my understanding and experience of Bodh Gaya and its potential is forever deepening and changing too. I know that as soon as I write things down, my understanding of Bodh Gaya will change again, and Bodh Gaya itself will also change. So all I am offering is a snapshot in time and place – an out-of-focus snapshot because I know that my vision will become clearer as I learn more.

This book had its beginnings in a talk I gave on our order convention held in Bodh Gaya for the first time in 2009. After giving the talk I thought I would feel satisfied that I had communicated myself, but actually I felt that what I had said was just the tip of the iceberg, and also that I wanted to communicate with the broader Buddhist world as well. I want to inspire all those in Bodh Gaya and beyond who cherish it as I do. I think that a stronger Bodh Gaya in the 21st century could mean a stronger, more effective Buddhism, and strengthening Buddhism's vitality and influence can only have a positive effect on the whole of humanity.

I cannot imagine a more meaningful mission than this, and I am humbled and full of joy at the prospect of serving the Buddha in this way. In my view, Bodh Gaya is at a crucial point, and there are many threats to its integrity. It is an insufficient response to just hope things will turn out OK; if we really want things to change in a positive direction, we must act to influence that change.

I will not try to write about Bodh Gaya's history, which is well documented elsewhere. I want to take a snapshot of Bodh Gaya now, to capture its spirit and significance in this time. I also want to help visitors to appreciate Bodh Gaya; the more you know about its significance, the more satisfying your visit will be.

May all beings be touched by the deep peace of the Buddha's realisation under the great bodhi tree.

Thanks

There are countless small conditions that have come together to support the creation of this book, and I am extremely grateful to many people for the help and support I have received whilst writing it. I especially want to thank Sarah, my partner, who has allowed me to work on this while she has looked after Archie, our little boy. She has given a lot of time and support, putting her own projects on hold while I've been writing. Without her this book would have been very difficult to complete.

Many thanks as well to all the people who allowed me to interview them for this book, including Bhante Sewali, head monk of the Maha Bodhi Society, Bodh Gaya; the 17th Gyalwang Karmapa, Tergar Monastery; Keiren Lama, who is responsible for the Dailokyo Temple; Nangzey Dorjee, the secretary of the Bodh Gaya Temple Management Committee; Shashi Kumar, director of the Bodhichitra thankga school in Bodh Gaya; Tenzin Thabkhey, head monk of the Dalai Lama's own temple in Bodh Gaya; 'Bodhitree Mike', an American who belongs to the Nyingma Vajrayana tradition; Christopher Titmuss, who is English by birth, went to Bodh Gaya for the first time in 1974 as a Thai monk and has been going there ever since; Maitrivir-Nagarjuna, a member of the Triratna Buddhist Order who is a lecturer in Buddhist aesthetics; Subhuti, a senior order member in the Triratna movement; and above all Sangharakshita, the founder of Triratna.

Also thank you to Buddhavajra and the Three Jewels Centre in Bodh Gaya, where I have spent time working on the book. I love working late at night, sometimes until 6 or 8 am. Working when the world is asleep is like being on a mini solitary retreat every day, and the imagination and energies flow. So thanks for letting me sleep in the mornings and helping with the printing. Thanks to my mum, dad and family and to the Padmaloka retreat centre. Thanks also to Priyananda from Windhorse Publications, to Vishvapani for his feedback, to Vidyadevi for taking on structuring and editing the book, and to Ruth Rudd for all her patience and expert help with typesetting. Thanks also to Jnanarakshita, Prajnananda, Guhyavajra, Padmavajra, Saddhaloka, Gordon Allan and Alice Archer for their help.

Quotations include passages from the Pali canon and the *Buddhacharita*, and also the memoirs of Anagarika Dharmapala; Sangharakshita's books, *A Survey of Buddhism*, *Moving Against the Stream*, *Crossing the Stream*, *What is the Sangha?*, *Complete Poems* and *The Rainbow Road*, all published by Windhorse Publications and his *Beating the Drum*, published by Ibis Publications; *Meeting the Buddha: On Pilgrimage in Buddhist India*, edited by Molly Emma Aitken, a Tricycle Book published by Riverhead Books, New York in 1995; *Noble Friendship*, by Khantipalo, published by Windhorse Publications; and *Gautama Buddha: the Life and Teachings of the Awakened One*, by Vishvapani, published by Quercus in 2011. Many thanks to the authors and publishers for kind permission to quote their work.

Editorial note

In the west the Buddha's teaching is often referred to as the Dharma, which is the Sanskrit term meaning 'way' or 'truth'. In Pali, the ancient language in which the Buddha's teaching was originally written down, the equivalent term is Dhamma. In this book we refer to the Buddha's teaching as the Dhamma, following the custom of the Triratna movement in India, who use Dhamma to denote the Buddhist meaning of the term, and to distinguish it from the Hindu use of the word *dharma*.

1

Introduction

Language and culture separate the Buddhist pilgrims; they follow different scriptures and view Gautama in diverse ways. Until western scholars made the suggestion, Buddhists in Sri Lanka and Japan had little sense that they shared a single religion – at least as the word has been understood in modern times; and, until those same scholars coined the word 'Buddhism', the faith had no single name. But all the pilgrims believe they are true heirs to Gautama's teaching (or perhaps to the spirit that informed it), and come to Bodh Gaya because of him.

Vishvapani, in *Gautama Buddha:
the Life and Teachings of the Awakened One*

Bodh Gaya is the place where Buddhism was born. It was here, more than 2,500 years ago, under a bodhi tree, that Siddhartha Gautama gained Enlightenment and thus became the Buddha. Today the very spot is marked by a bodhi tree and temple complex. The place is central to the Buddhist faith, for it symbolises the Buddha's realisation. Deep beauty and peace radiate from it – at least for those prepared to spend time soaking it up.

The temple site, which is about 400 metres square, is in the centre of Bodh Gaya village, sealed off from the village by a boundary wall with an entrance gateway in the market place. The complex, which has developed over many years, has hundreds of significant features: stone

1

stupas, trees, statues, symbolic images, small rooms, a lake, a meditation park, the main temple itself, many places to make offerings and room for candles. In its interest and intensity it is a place like no other.

The tree (together with the main temple that has developed around it) has been a focus for countless pilgrims and practitioners over the centuries. Bodh Gaya has had thousands of years of visitors all paying respect, honour, reverence and gratitude to this most significant place. In the 21st century, it not only connects us with the roots of Buddhism but also points the way to Buddhism's future. It has significance in many ways and on many levels. Like an ocean it has infinite depth and mystery.

There are dozens of monasteries, temples and Dhamma centres in and around Bodh Gaya, and the number is growing. They represent most of the world's Buddhist traditions, all drawn by the significance of this place. The village is crowded with pilgrims, meditators, Buddhist practitioners, tourists and Indians on holiday. Some western practitioners come every year, and some of them stay here for eight months of the year.

The Buddha is central to all Buddhist traditions, and the tree and temple symbolise his awakening, giving a unifying factor to the whole of Buddhism. We have come from all over the world to live and practise alongside each other, inspired by the Buddha's example. In Bodh Gaya, we have a chance to live beyond the limitations of our own approach to Buddhism. We have all come to India, where we are all fish out of water, away from our own culture and values, drawn by the tree which symbolises the great awakening and has the power to unify all traditions and 'hold' all of us here. In the 21st century this place gives a context in which as Buddhists we can re-examine our practice in the light of other traditions and see ourselves as a whole. Nowhere else in the world and at no other point in history have all the Buddhist traditions lived and practised together like this. Bodh Gaya thus offers a unique context for a great fusion of inspiration to take place.

I believe that this gathering of traditions, friendships, practice, festivals, culture and so much more – even forms of medicine and styles of cooking – gives us the right conditions for a renaissance of our ancient tradition. Many Buddhist traditions have taken up practice at Bodh Gaya with a passionate spirit. I believe that this is because we are all aware of its importance to us, or have an intuition that something is happening here. And here Sangharakshita, my own teacher, arranged for the purchase of a plot of land in 1993, at a time when countless other projects could have been given priority. He must have sensed it too. We – the Triratna Buddhist Community, founded in 1968 – have developed that land into what is now the Three Jewels Centre. We are beginning to take our place here, not just physically but in terms of mutual understanding and respect with the other Dhamma traditions based here.

Bodh Gaya is in some respects just like any other village in north-eastern India. Its busy market place is surrounded by fields full of crops, and the rhythm of its daily life is punctuated by Muslim calls to prayer, loudspeakers chanting mantras, the horns of cars, bikes and rickshaws, and occasionally the tribal drums of the funeral march beating out the rhythm of death, as mourners head towards the river bank with a corpse and some wood.

But if we approach Bodh Gaya with imagination and faith, we will get a sense of the aura of a world-changing event. The Buddha's influence radiates from this spot, and just a glimpse of the great bodhi tree brings delight to the hearts of all of us who have gone forth from worldly pursuits and taken refuge in the Buddha. This is our inheritance.

When you become a Buddhist you go through a process of dissolving interest in the mundane world. Reborn into the Buddha's family, you slowly let go of an old way of being and inherit a new world. You are now a son or daughter of the Buddha, and new vistas open up before you. This new world is jewel-adorned and full of beauty. Friendship is beautiful, meditation is beautiful, and hearing the teachings communicating truth is beautiful. We find significance in things that before we could only see in a limited way. As Buddhists we are inheritors of a deep and mysterious tradition, and we owe a great debt of gratitude to all those who helped bring it into our lives. We also have a responsibility and duty of care towards it. What we inherit is a treasure chest full to the brim with teachers and teachings, practitioners, places, meditations, Buddhas and Bodhisattvas. They all shine brightly, each uniquely radiant, light from each penetrating all the others.

In this treasure chest, Bodh Gaya is a radiant family jewel, even the 'jewel in the crown', a jewel that lights the whole world. In this book I would like to reach inside that great big family chest of ours and pull out this radiant jewel, lift it in the air and let the sun shine on it, so all of us can see its brilliance.

2

The story of
Siddhartha Gautama

*In search of what might be skilful, seeking the unexcelled state of
sublime peace, I wandered by stages in the Magadhan country
and came to the military town of Uruvela. There I saw some
delightful countryside, with an inspiring forest grove, a clear-
flowing river with fine, delightful banks, and villages for alms-
going on all sides. The thought occurred to me: 'How delightful
is this countryside ... This is just right for the exertion of a
clansman intent on exertion.' So I sat down right there.*

The Buddha describes his arrival in the place now
called Bodh Gaya, in the *Ariyapariyesana Sutta*

If we want to enter into the heart of Bodh Gaya, we must
go back in our imagination to a time when the whole area
was a jungle. From the legends that have grown up around
his life we gather that Siddhartha Gautama was a prince of
a very rich local tribe. He could have anything he wanted,
and was waited on hand and foot. In his palace he was
closed off from the world, and his father tried to keep
it that way, and did his best to shield his son from the
realities of life.

But something in the young man was not satisfied
with that, and one day he insisted on going out to see the
world. Legends say that he went out accompanied by his
charioteer, and saw someone lying on the ground writhing
in pain. He asked the charioteer, 'What has happened to
that man?' and he was told, 'That man is sick, sir.' 'And can

that happen to anyone?' 'Yes, anyone can get sick, and in many different ways.' Shocked and troubled, Siddhartha returned to his palace.

Then on another occasion, he saw a man who was very old, bent over with a stick to help him along. 'What has happened to him?' asked Siddhartha. 'He is old, sir. Everyone gets old, no one is immune.' Again deeply moved by what he had seen, Siddhartha returned to his palace.

On a third occasion, he saw a lifeless body being carried to a cremation ground. 'What is happening there?' he asked, and the charioteer said 'That person is dead, sir.' 'And does that happen to everyone?' 'Yes, everybody dies, no one is exempt.'

It was his response to his fourth journey out into the world, so say the stories, that decided Siddhartha's future. On this occasion he saw a man dressed in the rags of a homeless wanderer, carrying a begging bowl. And when he asked what the man was doing, the charioteer told him that this was a man who had left home in search of the truth about life.

These are what have always been known in the Buddhist tradition as the four sights, and of course we all see their equivalents around us every day – as no doubt Siddhartha did, sheltered life though he had been leading. But after he really saw the suffering of sickness, old age and death, something changed in him. He started to question: 'Why do people suffer, get old and die?' and he thought, 'I cannot just get on with my life knowing that all this suffering is there. What is its cause? Can it be overcome?'

Most of us, when we see these things, find a way of distracting ourselves from them – the usual tangle of relationships, work, entertainment, money, drink or drugs, endlessly distracting ourselves until we die. But Siddhartha did something radically different which changed his future and that of all humanity. He could not just get on with his life and accept humanity's fate. He had seen too much and felt compelled to act. And the fourth sight, the wandering holy man, had shown him what to do.

With many questions burning in his heart, he decided to leave his palace life in search of solutions. His quest was to find what was at the heart of suffering, and root out its cause for the sake of all beings. In the middle of the night he woke up, stood for a while and watched his family sleeping, silently said goodbye, and slid out of the house. He got rid of his princely clothes, cut off his hair off, picked up some old rags to wear and headed off into the jungle.

After a while Siddhartha met up with a teacher called Alara Kalama and asked him, 'What is your path to liberation?' Having been instructed, he started to try out the approach he had been taught. But after some time he realised that these practices did not lead to freedom. They were tranquil states of mind and no more. So he left and went on his way.

He found another set of practitioners whose teacher was called Uddaka Ramaputta and asked them if the teaching they were following led to liberation, happiness and freedom. They explained it to him and he spent some time practising with them, but again his heart was full of doubt. Finally concluding that their way was not the complete path to freedom, he left them to look for another path.

Next, he met up with some very hard-core ascetics whose method of spiritual practice was to torture and starve themselves. He spent many years doing these practices and became very proficient at them, but in the end he came to the conclusion that it had all been a waste of time. He was no closer to the complete freedom and happiness he was searching for. So he left them too, and walked alone.

He knew that he needed to find another way. His first priority was to stop starving himself and eat some food, and this was provided for him by a girl he met on the river bank who gave him some rice. When his body was filled with energy from eating the rice, he crossed the river, found a tranquil place to meditate, gathered some grass to form a seat, and sat down under the great bodhi tree in what became Bodh Gaya.

When he sat down, he said to himself, 'I vow that I will not get up from this spot until I have realised the deepest truth, and woken up in a freedom that cannot be lost, until I have been liberated from suffering's deepest causes.'

That night he engaged in the most important battle ever fought by a human being, a struggle which was for the benefit of all humanity. Some traditional pictures show him surrounded by forces trying to stop him from gaining Enlightenment; the traditional term for these forces is 'Mara'. He is attacked by demons and hideous creatures, but he is not afraid; he is surrounded by beautiful girls who try to tempt him, but he is not distracted. According to legend, arrows were fired at him, but when they reached his aura of light they turned into flowers and fell at his feet. Sitting there, with this great battle going on within him, Siddhartha held fast to his wish to become free, and despite Mara's best efforts, broke through all the bonds that held him, and won freedom.

Many statues of the Buddha show him with his right hand touching the earth, symbolising the defeat of Mara which was fundamental to Siddhartha's awakening. In the old stories the gesture recalls a further mythical aspect of the occasion. It is said that Mara mocked him, challenging him to prove that he had the right to sit in this place, to gain Enlightenment; and Siddhartha touched the earth, whereupon the earth goddess appeared, and bore witness to the many lifetimes of spiritual practice that had preceded this culminating moment. Nothing could now drag Siddhartha back into the rounds of endless suffering. No more would he be subject to all the things that cause grief and sadness, no longer would he be trapped in the cycle of limited existence, or tied down to this mortal world. He was a free man, free from habits, hatred and craving, free from the pain of the endless rounds of birth and death. The bonds of suffering had been broken. He was the Buddha, which means 'the one who is awake'.

He had won for himself and for all human beings the greatest of all possible victories. The doorway to total freedom was open at last. He was the pioneer who found and walked through that door, and he showed us the way. He became known as the Buddha, the awakened one. He was also the 'Tathagata', the 'thus-gone one', for he had 'gone beyond'. He was the 'Jina', the 'mighty conqueror', the 'Sugata', the 'happily gone', the 'Bhagavata', the enlightened one.

The Buddha straddles both historic and mythic realities, and his realisation is beyond words, but we can try to get a glimpse into his vast timeless world. The traditional descriptions from the Pali suttas give us some clues. He has 'extinguished the fires of craving through overcoming selfish desire'. He is 'solid and unshakable' – immovable peace. He has no anger, no pride, no fear, he is without grief, he is pure awareness, he is wisdom, infinite space. In a stormy sea he is the harbour of refuge, the cool cave, the island amidst the floods, the place of bliss, emancipation, liberation, safety, the supreme, the transcendental, the uncreated, the tranquil, the home of ease, the calm, the end of suffering, the medicine for all, the unshaken, the ambrosia, the immaterial, the imperishable, the abiding, the further shore, unending bliss, the bliss of effort, supreme joy, the ineffable, the detachment, the holy city.

The Buddha's efforts have to be seen within a very broad context. Long before modern space exploration showed us pictures of the galaxy, Buddhism said that there are millions of world systems throughout vast distances of space offering a truly cosmic perspective. The Buddhist tradition also relates to time as measured in uncountable billions of years. The Buddhist world-view tries to help us imagine infinity, stretching the limits of human imagination, breaking down the finite conception of time and space; and it sees the Buddha's Enlightenment within this context.

The world of man is in fact axial to all other planes of existence, from the 'highest' abode of bliss to the 'lowest' realm of suffering. This is due not merely to its intermediary position, or because the highest transcendental paths are attainable only on earth, but because in this world alone a Supreme Buddha can arise; and the diamond throne (the vajrasana) on which he sits for the rediscovery of the long-lost and long-forgotten way to Nirvana is regarded as the spiritual centre of the universe: it was the first spot to solidify when the earth arose out of the fire-mist at the beginning of the aeon, and at the end of the aeon it will be the last to pass away. The Buddha's attainment of Enlightenment has significance not for this world only but for the whole cosmos. He is, according to Pali texts, the teacher of gods no less than of men ...

... Gautama the Buddha, though historically a unique being, cosmologically speaking is but the latest scion of the Dynasty of the Buddhas. The historical context is itself contained within a context which coincides with the whole cosmos, with the immeasurable extent and duration of the entire world-system. Consequently the Buddha's discovery of the way to Nirvana is to be held as a rediscovery, and his proclamation of the Dharma a re-proclamation. Within

this infinitely enlarged context his attainment, far from being a unique occurrence, is the latest confirmation of a law which acts wherever and whenever conditions permit, and his teaching, far from being absolutely original, is new only in the sense that it is never out of date. The Dharma taught by the Buddha is termed in Pali sanatana, eternal, and akalika, timeless ... because it is the formulation in this Buddha-period of principles which are true in all times and in all places. It is not merely 'handed down' from one Buddha to another, like a family heirloom: all discover it afresh for themselves.

Sangharakshita, *A Survey of Buddhism*
pp.52–3, 64, 76

So this is the significance of Bodh Gaya. It is the place where Siddhartha Gautama's quest ended, the place where, for the first time in our world system, suffering was cut off at the root. This is the spot in this world where the doorway into the unconditioned opened, and it continues to be a symbol for that liberation. It is the *vajrasana*, the diamond throne.

After his Enlightenment, the Buddha stayed in Bodh Gaya for seven weeks, allowing his experience to unfold. That experience sent light waves throughout the universe that have touched the lives of millions throughout history and across the world.

3

The Buddha
touches my life

*Now this, monks, is the noble truth of suffering: birth is suffering,
aging is suffering, illness is suffering, death is suffering; union
with what is displeasing is suffering; separation from what is
pleasing is suffering; not to get what one wants is suffering;
in brief, the five aggregates subject to clinging are suffering.*

*Now this, monks, is the noble truth of the origin of suffering:
it is this craving that leads to renewed existence, accompanied
by delight and lust, seeking delight here and there; that is,
craving for sensual pleasures, craving for existence, craving
for extermination.*

*Now this, monks, is the noble truth of the cessation of
suffering: it is the remainderless fading away and cessation of
that same craving, the giving up and relinquishing of it, freedom from it, nonattachment.*

*Now this, monks, is the noble truth of the way leading to the
cessation of suffering: it is this Noble Eightfold Path.*

Dhammacakkapavattana Sutta, Samyutta Nikaya

My life is one of those that the Buddha has touched. I was
born in 1971 and lived all my early life in Plymouth. I
had a strong intuition that I had spent many lifetimes as
a warrior fighting in battles and that I would do that for
the last time in this life. Feeling I had to fight one last time,
at 16 years old I left home and joined the army. I spent a
year and a half in intensive training and then I joined the
Second Battalion of the Parachute Regiment. We did a few
months more specialist training and then I was posted

to Fermanagh in Northern Ireland. My next posting was to Kenya, to do some training in hot conditions in case we might have to fight in the First Gulf War, which was taking place at that time. Fortunately the war was over quickly and we never had to fight in it. During my time in the army, I was in Germany when the Berlin wall came down (although we were in a trench in a forest and saw nothing). My last posting was to Botswana, where we went for four months to help the local special forces fight against the poachers; this was by far my most ethical and enjoyable tour.

While I was there we went to Zimbabwe for a couple of weeks and unfortunately the jeep we were in had a serious accident. The back left tyre blew out and forced the vehicle to spin and then flip over, rolling a couple of times. I was squashed in the back, and the fuel went everywhere but luckily didn't catch fire. There were seven of us in the vehicle and five of us were injured. We contacted a local flying doctor and my friends made a runway for him to land on. The small plane took us to Botswana and there we caught a flight to the UK. Since the day of the accident I have been left with chronic pain in many parts of my back.

When the accident happened I was already in my final year in the army, as I had told them I wanted to leave. This was because I had read too many religious and philosophical books and had seen through the absurdity of being a soldier. I had become almost an objector within the ranks, mocking the system and just counting down the time before I left. After the accident I had ten months left in the army; I wasn't fit to work and just did light duties and lived in my VW camper van in the car park in between hospital visits, counting the days to freedom. When that day finally came I left Aldershot with the hope of a new life, joyful that I had completed my last duty as a habitual fighter.

I decided that I needed to live somewhere I didn't know anybody, so that I could make a new start. I wanted to be near the coast so I picked Ipswich off the map even though I'd never been there before. My camper van broke down 30 miles short, and after three weeks in a car park eventually I gave a bloke £20 and he towed my van to Ipswich. I parked my van on the docks, which had some life left in them but were largely run down, giving me a great free place to park. I lived there in my van for about two years, and read quite a few religious and philosophical books. I was interested in many different spiritual approaches and would go to different talks and meetings. At one point I said to myself that I would sit in my van and wouldn't leave till I got to the heart of one of the books I was reading, and after a couple of days I had insight or vision into it. Still looking for a spiritual home, one day I saw a poster for a Buddhist meeting so I went along. I felt an instant connection with the people, and the outlook made sense of my vision and gave a clear path of practice. The people exemplified to whatever extent they could what they were teaching. I felt that I had 'arrived home' and that I had been a Buddhist before in past lives.

Determined to live the Buddhist life wholeheartedly, I went to work for a team-based right livelihood business called Windhorse Trading based in Cambridge. I worked there from 1994 until 2003, but during that time a terrible crisis blew up in my family. My grandfather became mentally and physically abusive and unable to function normally, and he was put into a state mental institution where he continued to deteriorate. Whilst he was in there we got a letter from a distant relative from abroad asking us to look at the possibility that we might have Huntington's disease in our family. We looked at the medical dictionary which gave a description of the illness and instantly knew that my grandfather had it. The dictionary said that what he had was degenerative and terminal, which means that he would die from his condition. Even more worryingly, the dictionary said that the illness was hereditary and would be passed onto half of our family. We were left feeling both relieved and distraught. We felt relief that we knew what my grandfather had and could be patient and kind towards his condition, but we were petrified at the fate of our family. We now all had to come to terms with having a hereditary terminal illness. My Nan never knew about Huntington's because she died while my granddad was in hospital.

It is possible to have a test to see if you have inherited the defective gene which causes Huntington's. It is exactly 50/50 – half the children of someone with the disease inherit it and half don't. My mother and her three sisters and one brother had to decide whether or not to be tested, and eventually my mother, her brother and two of her sisters wanted to know. One by one they were tested and when the results came back my mother learned that she had inherited the gene, and so had my uncle and one of my aunts. Because my mother had got it, my two sisters and I had the test, and I was the one who had inherited the gene.

It was 1997 when I had the test, and I was preparing for ordination into the Triratna order. I realized I needed to go away somewhere alone so I could reflect. During my life I have always gone to the wilderness when I need some perspective. Whilst I was growing up and when I was in the army I often spent time alone up on Dartmoor or on the coast, just to have the rhythm of walking alone with a big space and my thoughts. This time, though, I needed more, so I went to the Himalayas in Nepal. The question of our mortality was burning in my stomach, and somehow I felt that I needed to be close to the Buddha to get some answers. So in the monsoon of 1998 I went to Bodh Gaya for a two month retreat, to sit at the feet of the Buddha and try to absorb his teaching. Thus I went directly to the source of the Buddha's Enlightenment.

I stayed with Siladitya at the Triratna centre (then in its very early days) for the rainy season and developed a strong daily routine of study and meditation. Every day I made offerings to the tree, and spent time reflecting on the four noble truths, which are:

1) Life has pain and suffering;
2) There is a cause and origin of that pain;
3) We can live free from pain and suffering;
4) There is a path of regular steps to take us away from pain to the state of mind free from suffering.

I also reflected on the three characteristics of conditioned existence (the *lakshanas*) – the Buddha's teaching which states that all compounded things are impermanent, insubstantial and involved in suffering.

I had a lot of time to reflect, letting me see these truths within my life experience. I had time to soak up the atmosphere, time to just sit around and absorb things. I spent time walking in the Buddha's footsteps, reflecting on my family's fate and the Buddha's vision. I spent hours in the presence of the great tree under which he gained his liberation, and sitting in the various places in which he spent time after his realisation. I looked with great gratitude at the noble bodhi tree, as the old texts describe the Buddha himself doing, and I stood by the Muchalinda lake, feeling its energy.

As I walked barefoot around the temple in the warm rain, watching the leaves and seeds being washed away from the tree and swept up by the monks, I could feel the purifying rain soaking into my being. Around the tree there is a deep beauty and peace, a calm and tranquillity. I felt its sacredness and the Buddha's presence. The tree was alert, vibrant and saturated with meaning. Its deep peace was a balm to my aching heart.

When I touched my head on the *vajrasana*, I met the Buddha personally for the first time. Something deep within me wanted to connect with my highest ideals. I realised that I had a deep need to unite with something substantial, to touch something meaningful, to taste something satisfying. I had had a long journey throughout my whole life and through the depths of my heart, and a long journey through Nepal and India to reach this point. I felt in touch with everything that had brought me to this place, all the practices I had done, all my efforts to meet the Buddha through my imagination, and through years of prostrations, meditations, pujas, visualizations, chanting, hearing stories and reading books, hearing his Dhamma and knowing his life.

All the devotion that had brought me to that spot welled up in me as I approached the tree. I felt perfectly alive. It was simple yet deeply profound. The Buddha's presence that had for so long lived in my imagination, all that I had built up in my heart, became living, breathing reality. Here, sitting in this very spot, Siddhartha woke up to the true nature of things. It was here that he attained Nirvana, this piece of ground now underneath my forehead.

Each time I go to sit by the tree at Bodh Gaya I find this event more and more mysterious. I imagine a simple man in rags walking to the tree and sitting down. He committed himself to waking up, went through a profoundly mysterious metamorphosis, and arose as the Buddha. Man and myth united. He was the embodiment of Nirvana, and at the same time he lived and breathed as I live and breathe. He was a man and I could feel his presence in different ways; he was historical and human, yet timeless and beyond the rounds of birth and death. Bodh Gaya is thus timeless too, a direct link beyond time and space to the unconditioned, to the Buddha's past, present and future.

Coming to this place has changed everything for me, ever since I first confronted my own version of the Buddha's four sights. I am extremely lucky in that I have a wonderful partner in Sarah. She is amazingly caring and considerate about my terrible back pain and also the fear that living with Huntington's disease brings. Huntington's dissolves away your functioning, from gentle symptoms at the start all the way to death. It takes away power and choice, it is humiliating, and it is hard to plan or predict how life will go. The symptoms are so diverse you never know which of them will strike and how they will affect you. One thing that is certain though is that time is marching on and the illness will consume me unless I die of something else first. My grandfather was the first to degenerate and die from the illness and after that my Aunt Jackie died in 2001 whilst I was being ordained. My Uncle Richard died in 2011, whilst I was in Bodh Gaya. My mum, Sue, has very advanced symptoms and with a great deal of support and care is still managing to live by herself. It won't be long until she needs to move into a more supported living situation.

I will be next, of course, and I have two children, Harriet, who is 18, and Archie, who is 5. They will have to face those challenges too. Archie is too young to be tested yet, and Harriet says she doesn't want to find out until she needs to know. At the moment doctors say I have about 2–5 % of the symptoms; their effect is very gentle, but there are many things I don't understand about how much the disease is affecting me. One problem I have is not knowing how long I will be able to function. The disease affects mental health as well as producing physical degeneration, so I could hit a wall of mental health problems which stops me from doing things. So far I am mostly OK, but I feel like I am walking on eggshells, because I don't know when and how it could all come crashing down. That is why I make very short term plans and think about what I can achieve this day, month or year.

My name, Nissoka, means 'without grief'. I really love this name and thank my dear friend and mentor Saddhaloka for giving it to me. If I lose touch with my inspiration I am instantly in a hellish state of mind. I can have a big 'pity party', thinking 'poor old me with this horrendous back pain and Huntington's disease in me and my family'. It is possible to sink into these states of mind for hours or even days. Because of this constant danger I am impelled to act swiftly with the precious time I have left.

One major cause of suffering is the fear of anticipation, fearing something that hasn't actually happened yet. This is one of my main problems as I wait for symptoms to come. One thing I have noticed is that the more I focus on my practice, the more grief, sadness and fear dissolve. They don't completely disappear but they take such a small place in my much bigger life and perspective. If I am for a time overwhelmed with grief then I know to just carry on with what I do and it will disappear or find perspective.

All of this is supported immeasurably by Bodh Gaya. The Buddha's example means that I know that it is possible to be completely free from grief, sadness and fear if I practise the path as he did. It gives me great confidence that this is a reality, not just an idea.

Grief is tied in with having a fixed and limited sense of self, and being here in Bodh Gaya dissolves that tiny sense of who I think I am and taps into an infinitely deeper dimension of being. This mythic dimension works in mysterious ways. I have no idea how grief, fear and sadness drop away, but they do, and I am left feeling deeply content.

4

A place
of pilgrimage

After ten years of perseverance, I succeeded in obtaining the consent of the Government for the erection of a comfortable rest-house for Buddhist pilgrims at Bodh Gaya. It consisted of ten rooms, an assembly-hall that would hold five hundred persons and a big corridor built like a cloister. There were baths, where weary pilgrims who had come from afar could refresh themselves, and a kitchen, where poor travellers could cook the food they had brought with them. The two or three resident monks and I were happy to minister to the material and spiritual needs of the five or six annual pilgrims from all parts of Asia. We never felt solitary; nor did we miss the activities of the outside world in that quiet grove that had witnessed the spiritual triumph of Gautama.

Anagarika Dharmapala describes the
rest-house he built in Bodh Gaya in 1901

Bodh Gaya has been a place of devotion and pilgrimage for more than 2,500 years. Over the centuries, inspired men and women, drawn by the gravitational pull of the diamond throne where the Buddha awoke, have made great efforts to come to this sacred place and place their heads upon it. They have given their faithful hearts, made offerings and sat with awe, sitting with the great gratitude that fountains in the heart of anyone touched by the Buddha's awakening.

Whether in earthly forms or in myth, hosts of great beings have paid homage here, along with millions of simple devoted hearts, and when we tap into this, we can imagine the spiritual community of past and present and feel their faith, humility and joy. There are countless stories of pilgrims journeying to Bodh Gaya.

The Tibetan Buddhist tradition imagines the Three Jewels of all Buddhist traditions – the Buddha, the Dhamma, his teaching, and the Sangha, the community of Buddhist practitioners – in the form of a 'refuge tree', in whose branches are to be seen all the teachers and inspirational figures associated with that particular tradition. My own order, the Triratna Buddhist Order, has its own refuge tree, symbolising the lineage from which Triratna has emerged. It is like our family tree, and some of the best-known pilgrims to Bodh Gaya are to be seen on it, so that at Bodh Gaya our family tree comes to life. On our refuge tree, for example, is Hsuan-tsang, the 7th-century Chinese monk and scholar who came to Bodh Gaya on a 16-year pilgrimage from China. His journal paints beautiful images, and Bodh Gaya was the highlight of his journey:

> Rare trees with their renowned flowers connect their shade and cast their shadows; the delicate sha herb and different shrubs carpet the soil. The principal gate opens to the east, opposite the Nairanjana river. The southern gate adjoins a great flowery bank. The western side is blocked up and difficult of access. The northern gate opens into the great sangharama. Within the surrounding wall the sacred traces touch one another in all directions. Here there are stupas, in another place viharas. The kings, princes, and great personages throughout all Jambudvipa, who have accepted the bequeathed teaching as handed down to them, have erected these monuments as memorials.

Also on our refuge tree is Shantideva, the renowned 8th-century Indian scholar of Mahayana Buddhism; he was based at the great Buddhist university at Nalanda, just 90 km from Bodh Gaya, and must surely have come here to gain inspiration. Nagarjuna, the exponent of the Perfection of Wisdom, was an abbot at Nalanda, and must have come here on pilgrimage too. Sangharakshita, the founder of our movement, has been here many times. Here he describes his first ever visit:

Bodh Gaya! Bodh Gaya! How many people have come to you in the course of ages! How many pilgrim feet have trodden the dust of your groves, how many pairs of hands been joined in silent adoration beneath the wide-spreading boughs of the Tree of Enlightenment, how many heads touched in profound thanksgiving the edge of the Diamond Throne! Bodh Gaya! Bodh Gaya! How beautiful you are in the morning, with the sunlight streaming on the renovated façade of your great temple as it rises four-square against the cloudless blue sky! How beautiful in the evening, when in the shadowy depths of the deserted temple courtyard a thousand votive lamps glitter like reflections of the stars! Bodh Gaya, I shall always remember how beautiful you were the first time I saw you, when my heart was young, and you made me your own!

(*The Rainbow Road*)

Anagarika Dharmapala, who is on the tree of refuge and respect imagined by Triratna members in India, is one of the most important figures in the revival of Buddhism in modern India. He was born in Sri Lanka (then Ceylon) in 1864 and became a Buddhist monk; and in 1891 he visited Bodh Gaya and found his life's work. He wrote of that first visit:

After driving six miles (from Gaya) we arrived at the holy spot. Within a mile you could see lying scattered here and there broken statues etc, of our blessed Lord. At the entrance to the Mahant's temple on both sides of the portico there are statues of our Lord in the attitude of meditation and expounding the Law. How elevating! The sacred Vihara – the Lord sitting on his throne and the great solemnity which pervades all round makes the heart of the pious devotee weep. How delightful! As soon as I touched with my forehead the vajrasana a sudden impulse came to my mind. It prompted me to stop here and take care of this sacred spot – so sacred that nothing in the world is equal to this place where Prince Sakya Sinha gained Enlightenment under the bodhi tree.

This he did, and as part of that great effort he founded the Maha Bodhi Society, whose aim was to restore Bodh Gaya, which had been much neglected, to its former splendour.

Dhardo Rimpoche, one of Sangharakshita's Tibetan teachers during the time he lived in the Himalayan town of Kalimpong, was an abbot in Bodh Gaya for many years, and Dr B.R. Ambedkar, the great 20th-century hero who helped bring Buddhism back to India, also came here.

According to Tibetan legend, Padmasambhava, a figure who straddles both historic and mythic realities, was ordained a monk at Bodh Gaya, and defeated the Hindu pundits in debate and magic, thus saving the *vajrasana* for Buddhism. So both historically and mythically, Bodh Gaya is at the heart of our tradition. When we come here, we don't just take our place in history. We open up a whole dimension of Sangha, woven from the golden threads of history and myth, a worldly stage, a place of pilgrimage with a timeless blessing which permeates and saturates the very earth here. It radiates from the tree and rustles in the leaves. Anyone prepared to sit here and open up to its infinite space and

peace can access it. It lives in the people who practise
the Buddha's way. If you come here, you can sense his
victory everywhere: in the leaves of the tree and in the
hearts of the genuine-hearted community.

5

Reflections on the Tree

Even on that still afternoon each individual, heart-shaped leaf, with its long-drawn, tapering tendril tip, was trembling and spinning on its slender foot-stalk, until the whole tree was in agitation – every one of the myriad glossy, green leaves with a separate light as these thousands of perpetually moving mirrors caught the sun. The restlessness and activity of these bo-leaves, vibrating and striking together with a tinkling noise like the patter of soft raindrops on still nights, make the pipul the most grateful shade-tree, and the reflections of its glossy leaves suggest always the first stir of a rising breeze. This flashing, sparkling, flickering play of light all over the tree gives the pipul its unique and individual character – something like the dazzling, glittering trees that one sees in pictures by imperfect vitascope. The pipul trembles to this day in reverence for the one who became Buddha beneath its branches, and as symbol of continual change and motion, the impermanency of the world.

Elizabeth Ruhamah Scidmore describes a visit to the bodhi tree in 1903 (quoted in *Meeting the Buddha: on pilgrimage in Buddhist India*)

When visiting Bodh Gaya, different people connect with different aspects of the temple complex. Some relate to the bodhi tree, some the *vajrasana*, the 'diamond throne' where the Buddha sat, some the lofty spire of the main temple, some the Buddha's footsteps or the lotus tank. The actual spot where the Buddha is said to have sat is now occupied by the big temple where the statue is, the *vajrasana* being a symbolic representation of the spot.

The complex is a wonderful place to explore; you find new things all the time. Even after coming here for many years I still find new ways to deepen my relationship with the place. To give one small example, just outside the temple is a jungle garden next to the Mahant's house by the river. It is full of trees, and gives the sense of peace and contentment that comes when one is in nature just enjoying it for its own sake. When I am there I feel that of all the areas in Bodh Gaya, it is probably the closest to being like the jungle that was there when the Buddha-to-be chose to come here and sit down all those years ago. Going to the busy market I often wonder whether Siddhartha would come here now to strive for Enlightenment, with all the horns blaring, market-stall holders shouting and amplified music. I doubt it very much; I think he'd find a jungle elsewhere.

For me, the most significant thing here is the bodhi tree. The tree that is at present in the Mahabodhi temple courtyard is said to be a direct descendant from the original tree under which the Buddha sat, probably the fourth or fifth generation. The bodhi tree (or bo tree, from the Sinhalese *bo*) is a species of fig tree, and of course it is called 'bodhi' because underneath it the Buddha achieved Enlightenment or *bodhi*. The Jataka stories of the early Buddhist tradition record the Buddha himself as saying that bodhi trees should be regarded as places of veneration, as representative of the Buddha himself: 'The great bo-tree used by the Buddhas is fit for a shrine, be they alive or be they dead', the *Kalinga-bodhi-jataka* says. In early Buddhist history, the Buddha himself was not depicted in visual art; instead, the bodhi tree was used to represent his presence.

The tree is a perfect symbol to be at the heart of Buddhism. Trees are majestic and regal; they give confidence, they have character and grace. A tree does not get involved in tribal bickering and division, it is not plagued by partisan desire. It is like having a wise old friend you can talk to. And it is a deep symbol of unity because many branches come from one trunk. The bodhi tree is a symbol of greatness and strength. It stands strong and radiant, as if it knows it is at the heart of a great and noble lineage. Saturated with peace and with nothing to prove, its presence offers a vision of unity beyond words.

Trees are a symbol of what has been here in the past, our history and roots, and yet they also symbolise growth for the future. A tree has energy, dynamism and grace. Trees support us, we take refuge under them and they protect us from storms. They teach us the need for deep roots; the deeper the foundation the taller one can grow. If we look carefully at a tree's various limbs held high, reaching out in different directions, we see that all of them rejoice in their own individuality. Each limb has its own beauty, but all the limbs come from the powerful trunk, all the branches from one mighty foundation, just as all Buddhist schools come from one original source, the Buddha.

This central foundation is rooted in the earth, so deeply that it is almost of the earth itself. Its greatness is born from the confidence coming from its own deep roots, like the Buddha's confidence expressed in the earth-touching gesture, which says, 'My great liberation is born from the deepest foundation of truth.'

The Dhamma is part of nature, and the man or woman who seeks and achieves Enlightenment is in tune with the fundamental structure of the universe. When Siddhartha became the Buddha, his Enlightenment was witnessed and confirmed by the earth goddess, whose nature is based in the very fabric of things.

Each tree is a powerful symbol of the true individual. Through its own efforts, each tree stands by itself, and yet it can stand in a forest with others. If you think of the Sangha as a forest, you will see that there are many different types of trees, but all rely on the sun, rain and air. In the same way, there are many different types of Buddhist traditions that grow in the Sangha forest, yet all of these grow from the Three Jewels: Buddha, Dhamma and Sangha.

The tree as a symbol is not religious or dogmatic. It is open to everybody. You don't need to be Buddhist to relate to a tree. It is a universal symbol. There are wise old trees all over the world; in every country, people sit under them and feel at peace and in touch with the earth. We may also feel in touch with our ancestry because of the tree's great age.

If there is a tree that you love – not necessarily an officially sacred tree, perhaps just one in your own garden or a nearby park – when you sit under it you can feel that you are in communication with a friend. You feel protected by its power and grace. You can touch it with your hands and arms, maybe place your head on it and feel its wise old heart. Deep in the memory of the tree at Bodh Gaya is the peace, wisdom and compassion of Shakyamuni, and we can feel his presence. His liberation that day created an impression so powerful that it resonates today. Thousand of years have passed and yet time has stood still.

Old trees bring a sense that they reach back beyond our small and insignificant lives. Billions of people have lived and died, and the tree at Bodh Gaya is still strong. It has seen human fortunes rise and fall, just as it has witnessed Buddhism's rise, fall and rise again. A tree symbolises longevity and strength. Paradoxically, it also symbolises impermanence. As we see the branches sagging down and falling off, we witness decay and death taking hold of this sacred symbol. The tree has something to teach us about the characteristics of conditioned life. Nothing is free from impermanence; it too is subject to decay and death just as we all are. It offers us that reflection and possible insight into the nature of existence. The Buddha himself felt great gratitude towards the tree in whose shelter he experienced the interconnectedness and interdependence of things.

The bodhi tree is a companion in daily life and a true *kalyana mitra* (a spiritual friend). If I am having a bad day or experiencing a negative state of mind, I go and sit under the tree, and the peace, energy and imagination emanating from it dissolve away these feelings, as a bigger perspective arises. I have no idea how this works – it seems like magic! – but over many years I have developed a very strong relationship with the tree in this way. It is a place where the Buddha's qualities can enter deeply into your heart and mind. Trees have 'memories' too; they are holders of our history in a literal sense. If we slice open a tree to reveal its rings and marks, it can tell us a story about time. And as we have seen, a 'refuge tree' tells the story of our Dhamma history.

I do Chi Kung and in that we are asked to be like a tree, to embody and invoke the spirit of a tree. We imagine its qualities and are asked to emulate them: solid, grounded, rooted in the earth. I have a video of my instructor performing Chi Kung in front of a 4,000 year old tree. It's an easy metaphor to connect with, stimulating the imagination to understand qualities of rootedness, grace, statis and dynamism.

Static and dynamic are usually contradictions but when we sit under the bodhi tree we are challenged to accept them, not prematurely trying to come up with an intellectual answer, but just sitting there with the contradictions and opening up the mystery.

6

The Buddha Peace

The world can whir and hum and crank on with its noisy business, and yet the stillness is there. The peace is within. Prostrations and chanting and supplication and prayer clogged the air and yet that cool, empty space beneath that tree remained untouched. The Buddha still sat there, as he did twenty-five hundred years ago, with eyes closed and attention turned inward.

Eric Lerner, describing a visit to the
bodhi tree in 1972 (quoted in *Meeting the
Buddha: on pilgrimage in Buddhist India*)

When I'm sitting near the bodhi tree at Bodh Gaya I sense a paradox. Peace can coexist with noise here. The temple can be very busy, with people coming and going, chanting, talking. There are dogs wandering through, people making offerings, big groups listening to talks, people taking photos, groups doing pujas. There is so much movement and noise, and yet somehow there is still a deep, deep sense of peace.

This peace is a doorway into the unconditioned. It is steeped in wisdom and compassion, tranquil yet filled with energy. It is boundless and radiates love; it burns with the intense fire of transformation. It tastes of freedom, for samsara's bonds were broken at this very spot. It is the profound peace of a broken 'self,' 'seen through' or 'gone beyond'. It is powerful and dynamic and infused with insight and liberation. It is a peace that dissolves fear and doubt, a peace that rejoices in the conquest of Mara, a peace that celebrates and is full of joy at Siddhartha's great victory. It breaks down the boundaries of time and space, it is selfless and transcends all dualities, it is empty and dwells in the void. It has a power, magnitude and solidity like no other place on earth.

When Aung San Suu Kyi was accepting her Nobel peace prize she described peace as 'the beneficial coolness that comes when a fire is extinguished', a powerful image that helps us to understand that peace comes when samsara's painful fires are put out and peace is left. It is not that we extinguish ourselves; we just realise that there is nothing there to begin with, nothing fixed or permanent.

The Buddha peace is nothing to do with ideas, but a deep spiritual reality, and that reality can be felt around the bodhi tree. The peace and emptiness at the *vajrasana* is of 'another world'. It is as if we are in the presence of something beyond our limited world, and we sit waiting for a clue as to what inhabits that deep emptiness and peace.

Peace is much deeper and more profound than simple silence. Silence is just the lack of noise. Many places in the world have no noise, but they don't have a sense of peace like that of the bodhi tree, where peace and noise can coexist. Of course, it is deeply satisfying when there is silence there, and I feel that silence should be observed as much as possible around the tree for the benefit of everybody, but even when there is no silence, peace can still be felt.

Sometimes at the temple I am reminded of a beach. It's as though we are all sitting around looking out to sea, perhaps at a beautiful sunset, appreciating and admiring it, and occasionally looking round at the other people on the beach, just taking in and soaking up a sense of beauty and meaning.

Most evenings I do a puja around the bodhi tree, and no two are ever the same. It is not like the contained, quiet and protected pujas we do in shrine rooms in the UK. Under the tree you get dogs, children, gatherings of monks, tourists with video cameras, pilgrims and locals, processions, masses of people making offerings, people sitting meditating with you, tourists looking at you, Dhamma talks. It is a complex symphony of sounds, chanting, songs, conversations, and even megaphones.

At first I used to think 'It's too noisy to do any practice here', but as I listened closely I realised I could distinguish some familiar chants and sounds, and then I recognised that within the noise there were things that I could connect with. In the general hubbub there are always things I feel a kinship with, things I do myself but in a different way. Then the penny drops and I realise that we are *all* worshipping the Buddha. The other people there aren't getting in 'my' way; we are a choir of individuals and traditions, an ongoing chorus to which we all take our turn to add our voices and hearts. It is a 24-hour puja, and we can play our part in this ongoing celebration.

Meditating and reflecting are also offerings. The temple is a hub of practice and effort, with everyone taking refuge in all our many different ways and on our many different levels. Through its loud overt offerings and silent full-hearted prayers and intentions, Bodh Gaya is a place of great joy, harmony and depth, and there are lots of smiles all round. If Bodh Gaya is a symphony of practice, just like being in a choir or orchestra, being there requires both action and receptivity. Listening to and witnessing each other, we have the chance to experience a collective resonance. Sometimes we may be taking part in pujas while others watch us, and sometimes we are witnessing the practice of others, but witnessing is also taking part.

Joining practice here, we pound our 'self' with daily ritual, breaking down the self to realise the connectedness of all. When we meet Buddhists from all over the world and chant mantras and do pujas together, we feel united and harmonised in the deepest aspects of our individual and collective consciousness. If you attend a Dhamma centre in your own country, you may have experienced the joy of gathering together to practise on festival days. Imagine that sense of connectedness with other parts of the whole Buddhist tradition!

Mutual delight is ever-present around the tree, the delight of the beautiful community of practitioners, sympathetically enjoying one another's presence. Here we can touch upon the 'fragrance of the perfect life, sweeter than incense', to use words from a puja I often recite. Even though we don't speak the same language, so much communication goes on: smiles, little gifts, generosity and help.

The temple is a non-sectarian open space. Bodh Gaya is unbiased, and the tree is always open to everybody. Not even the Dalai Lama can book the spot under the tree and close the whole temple. If you want to go to the temple and wave bananas over your head and bounce around on one leg, go ahead, if that's your practice! Of course mostly people chant and meditate, but choice and freedom is always there. As Mr Dorgee, the Secretary of the Temple Management Committee that looks after the temple, says, 'There are very few rules at the temple'. People are free to express themselves as they wish, which is very liberating. It's a good environment in which to express yourself without inhibition.

The meeting together of the different Buddhist traditions in Bodh Gaya often presents the sublime and the ridiculous in the same moment. Sitting under the tree one can simultaneously feel a deep sense of unity and mutual appreciation with a number of people and at the same time be confronted by the bellowing through a megaphone of someone with little or no awareness of others. Although at its best Bodh Gaya can connect you to a sense of mutual delight, it can also leave you feeling shocked disbelief at what some people are capable of doing. But this shocking dimension of a multi-layered experience need not deter us from going to the temple and working with whatever feelings arise, although we may also want to make the most of the situation by getting to know which times of day are likely to be quieter.

In the village surrounding the temple, my sense is that there is a general feeling of peace. Buddhism has had a strong positive influence on it, I would say. I think all towns and cities have a certain 'vibe' or 'spirit'. London, to my mind, is anxious and spiritually empty, while in Kathmandu in Nepal I had a strong sense of a kind of magic resonating in all the people. And to me Bodh Gaya feels deeply peaceful, with a sense of celebration and joy, as well as a weighty feeling of gravity because a world-changing event happened here.

Everyone can come and partake in the Buddha's great peace. Many people who visit here remark on its effect on them – not just Indian visitors or just Buddhists, but people of all faiths from all over the world. Anyone can come and explore the temple, and they are made to feel welcome.

Local people also love the temple. It is a real asset to the village, and lots of residents go there to sit and talk peacefully, even though most of them are Hindu or Muslim. Peace is a universal principle which everyone can relate to. I have seen Indian soldiers spinning prayer wheels at the temple. Even when the compound is heaving with thousands of people and it's impossible to move, the crowds are friendly. Nitish Kumar, the governor of Bihar, said he was 'happy because he never needs much security

in Bodh Gaya because of the atmosphere here'. That feeling
of friendliness and peace is present in the numerous cafes
and tea shops scattered all over Bodh Gaya. All faiths, all
traditions, all countries, all races, are welcome to feel the
peace of the Buddha in this place.

7

Unity at
Bodh Gaya

*I listen to the chanting, surrendering to the deep silence that
underlies it. I am so grateful to be here, for I understand that
no matter how different we may appear, in skin colour and size
and costume, all of that falls away before the flame of shared
humanity that burns in us, our potential for enlightened mind.*
Sandy Boucher, 1991 (quoted
in *Meeting the Buddha*)

The Buddha's great victory broke the bonds that held him
and the world in a never-ending cycle of painful existence.
Imagine for a moment the seat of his liberation, the great
vajrasana, as a throne of pure diamond, shining with the
light of his timeless realization. The Buddha communicated
his great awakening to others and they in turn were
illuminated. They also communicated the way, and the next
generation were illuminated too. In this way the Buddha's
light was passed on from one generation of disciples to
another. To start with, there was only a faint glimmer,
but eventually a whole stream of light emerged. Many
different Buddhist schools and traditions have come into
being, and they have spread through history and across the
globe, each arising in response to the needs and customs of
whatever culture, context or nation it encountered. From
this one spot, Buddhism has been embraced by millions
all over the world.

Ever since the Buddha's Enlightenment Bodh Gaya has been a place of pilgrimage, but in the last fifty years something magical has started to happen. The fragments of light that were spread all over the world are now coalescing back in Bodh Gaya. Buddhist traditions from many countries now have centres here; they have come back to the root source of the Buddha's original breakthrough. His Enlightenment is the essence of the light that shines from all these traditions, though now it is now expressed in so many different ways.

In Buddhism we don't have a Pope or a Vatican, or a text that is the central authority to defer to like a Bible. There are no commandments. There is really no authority or power at all, just the example of the Buddha and his Enlightenment. All Buddhists accept that the Buddha attained Enlightenment and taught the path to Enlightenment, all schools of Buddhism derive their doctrines and methods from the Buddha's Enlightened vision, and all those doctrines and methods are aimed at attaining Enlightenment. The practices come from the Buddha or those inspired by him. For example, even though Padmasambhava is a strong focus for some traditions in Tibet, the Buddha is still at the tradition's root.

This daily connection with the historical Buddha is a very basic and practical thing which keeps reminding us of this solidarity. Whether you're from a small gompa high in the Himalayas, a Thai forest monastery or a Triratna Buddhist centre, it is through the Buddha that you can unite with others and potentially find harmony. Our focus on the historical Buddha helps us to keep that perspective.

All schools of Buddhism aim at Enlightenment, at repro-ducing the spirit and experience of the Buddha. This unity is not rational but transcendental. That is to say the doctrinal and other differences between the schools are

*not resolved by being reduced on their own level one to
another or all to a conceptual denominator, but transcended
by referring them to a factor which, being supra-logical,
can be the common object of contradictory assertions. ...
This is not to say that doctrinal differences were not keenly
felt and vigorously debated, or that sectarian feeling did
not sometimes run high; but such differences were always
settled peacefully, by means of discussion, no attempt ever
being made to enforce conformity. Persecution, or 'arguing
by torture', was unknown. Neither was anyone consigned
to hell by his opponent for holding unorthodox views. ...
Between the different schools of Buddhism there was a
relationship of mutual respect and tolerance.*

Sangharakshita in *A Survey of Buddhism*, p.8

As Sangharakshita told me in an interview, 'Unity can
happen if the different Buddhist schools and traditions
recognize that Enlightenment is their true goal and have
a path to achieve that, and if they acknowledge that in
principle all the different traditions of Buddhism have
that as their aim.'

In another context, Sangharakshita emphasized that this
recognition should not just be intellectual but heartfelt. In
a paper called *Extending the Hand of Fellowship* he says: 'The
Triratna [the Buddhist order he founded] is a branch of the
mighty tree of Buddhism which, for more than 2,500 years,
has sheltered a considerable portion of humanity, and the
same vital juice that circulates in the older, bigger branches
of the tree circulates in our younger, smaller branch too,
even if it circulates in it a little more vigorously than it
does in some of them. It is important that we should not
only acknowledge this intellectually but also *feel* it.' Bodh
Gaya gives us a unique opportunity for feeling it. Here
Buddhism is not from a textbook or in pictures. Here our
Dhamma practice is not conducted through email or in

stuffy meetings. Here we *feel* the presence of the Buddha and we *feel* the Sangha together.

A woman from a nation I cannot pin down sits on a step under the bodhi tree and quietly does her afternoon prayers, gently wishing for the Buddha's vision to open up in her heart and mind. Her soft voice is enchanting and lifts a deep-hearted smile in me. I am filled with joy to hear someone communicating with the Buddha so sincerely. She then cleans the base of the *vajrasana* with a cloth. When she finishes her beautiful chant she packs away her bag and bows several times to the Buddha, her head pushed to the floor for a long time in reverence. She sits up with her hands folded, absorbing her experience, then puts her multi-coloured bag over her shoulder, takes a white flag from it and offers it to the tree.

I don't know where she is from or what she is chanting, but that doesn't matter – we are deeply bonded through our love of the Buddha. As she passes we smile at each other as if we are friends. She is closer than a sister to me because of our common taking refuge and yet I don't know her race, her caste, her birthplace, her age, her education, her title, her status, her occupation, whether she is married, or anything about her. Most of the time we place far too much importance on these things. I know nothing about her and yet we have a bond. There are often westerners taking photos near the tree, just passing through, but even though they are from the same cultural background as me, I do not feel the deep bond with them that I feel with Dhamma practitioners, wherever they are from.

Around Bodh Gaya, all the monasteries fly the same flag; it represents all of Buddhism, and was first hoisted on Wesak Full Moon Day in 1885. (Wesak, the full moon of the month of May, is the festival day celebrating the Buddha's Enlightenment.) The flag is used throughout the world, having been accepted as the international

Buddhist flag by the 1952 World Buddhist Congress. Its stripes are blue, yellow, red, white and orange, the colours of the aura said to have emanated from the body of the Buddha when he attained Enlightenment under the bodhi tree. The different colours represent the qualities of the Dhamma – loving kindness, the middle path, the blessings of practice, the purity of the Dhamma and the Buddha's teachings. One account of the flag's symbolism says that the horizontal stripes represent the races of the world living in harmony and the vertical stripes represent eternal world peace. I think it's a good sign that all of the temples around Bodh Gaya identify with the flag and what it represents; it seems to show that we are Buddhists first and foremost, rather than here to represent our own tradition or country.

Relics said to be those of the Buddha and two of his chief disciples, Moggallana and Sariputta, are stored in the Maha Bodhi Society, and every couple of years they are paraded around Bodh Gaya on elephants. Hundreds of Buddhists create a procession, and thousands of people join in, to make a spectacle of colour, delight and unity. Christopher Titmuss, an English Buddhist teacher who has held a yearly retreat at Bodh Gaya since 1975, said: 'The best way to create unity in Bodh Gaya is the coming together on festival days, and the kind of events that bring the various traditions together in cooperation.' Living together harmoniously is an ideal not just for Buddhists but for the whole of humanity. It is our challenge in the 21st century to rise up to this vision.

We need to leave tribal thinking, politics, dogma and attachment to identity and differences at the gate outside the temple complex. We can just enter it and enjoy that simple feeling of interconnectedness through our appreciation for the Buddha and for the great assortment of people who come here. It is important to realise that we are not in competition with each other. We do not negate each other, but complement each other.

Nowhere else in the world today, and at no time in history, have all the traditions of Buddhism lived and practised side by side as they do at Bodh Gaya. Sometimes there are Buddhist conferences in different parts of the world, but these tend to be a coming together of ideas rather than an opportunity to live and practise together. Talking shops are limited, in my view, because words can only go so far. Bodh Gaya gives us the first real opportunity for a true Buddhist fusion to take place. But we can't just gather together and hope it will work out. What will unify us is a shared heartfelt connection with the historical Buddha and his Enlightenment, and a direct sense that he is central in our lives. If we relate to each other through this deep bond, harmony will thrive. There is a time for discussion and a time to experience unity by practising alongside each other. In the temple we have a chance to let go of our 'positions'. We can pick up the debate another day. Around the bodhi tree we all worship as Buddhists, beginning to soften boundaries of culture, tradition, geography and race. The Buddha's Enlightenment is central to all traditions, and the bodhi tree's presence unifies us all.

8

The great Buddhist melting pot

I returned [to the bodhi tree] as early as I could the next morning. I was not the first one there. Tibetan monks in their rough red robes were doing prostrations on shiny well-worn wooden boards pointed in the direction of the temple and tree, along with a scattering of Westerners dressed in sweatpants and T-shirts. Tibetans, Bhutanese and Ladakhis wearing dusty chubas spun prayer-wheels and fingered beads; Thais, Sinhalese, and Burmese laymen and women walked in silent contemplation or animated conversation. Japanese in white shirts and dark trousers walked briskly and snapped photos.

Rick Fields visits the bodhi tree in 1990,
quoted in *Meeting the Buddha*

Striving for unity doesn't mean suspending our critical faculties and stopping challenging each other. Healthy debate is vital to the life of the spiritual community. We just need to have our discussions in a spirit of being open to debate, rather than with a view to reinforcing our own tradition. Practising alongside each other brings up many questions. You may be challenged to ask yourself, 'What do I aspire to? And do all the practitioners here aspire to the same thing?' We all have criticisms of each other's traditions and that is part of a healthy Sangha. We cannot be expected to accept things blindly; the Buddha warned us against that and advised us to test things out in our own experience. Unity is not about agreeing with each other all the time, it's about being able to hold different views and still relate to each other through dialogue and understanding. We really need both parts of the relationship. If we lose our critical faculty, we run the risk of accepting things without question, but if we focus solely on the things that divide us, we risk division, separation and disharmony. Bodh Gaya gives us a chance to experience both sides. When I discussed this with Christopher Titmuss, he said: 'Bodh Gaya is the only place where all these traditions actually get together in the same locality consistently … and therefore it can be an enormous melting pot, a discussion point, a transforming point. It is a vitally important place for all traditions to talk, not too caught up in the divisive, judgemental self-righteous views which are the nightmare of all religions.'

There are over forty permanent monasteries here, and there are more each year. Each one represents its own tradition and country of origin, and they have amazing diversity and grandeur. There are also dozens of smaller Buddhist communities, and guesthouses to accommodate the pilgrims, practitioners and devotees who flock to this place, among them many western regulars who come here each year, each with their own purpose. Some are connected to specific Buddhist traditions and others are not, but they tend to come in the winter and leave in March when it starts to get too hot. On top of that you get pilgrims from Buddhist countries who flood Bodh Gaya in waves of the various colours related to their own traditions.

A big soup

We can imagine Bodh Gaya as a big stew or soup full of vegetables and spice. This soup has one taste – not the taste of salt or even garam masala, but the taste of freedom, a truly universal flavour. But although the soup has one taste, we are all separate ingredients; we don't expect the carrot to become a potato, or peas to become carrots, but their different textures and flavours complement each other.

To take the soup idea a bit further, hunger is universal, but even if back in our home country potatoes are the staple diet, not everybody eats potatoes to satisfy their hunger. Some people eat peas or carrots. Different flavours suit different people. Why should we cling to the idea that only 'our' potatoes can be truly satisfying? If we do this, we mistake the potato for the sense of satisfaction. We may even start thinking that the potato is the only 'real' vegetable, and that satisfaction 'is' a potato.

All the traditions are not going to be blended into one another in a big watery soup. They will keep their individual characteristics, though over time they may pick up the spirit or flavour of each other. Far from wanting unity to be a bland soup, we can rejoice in and enjoy our differences. It is great that there are different traditions; that way, between us we can reach more people. Not everyone is attracted to the same way of doing things, so diversity based on unity is strength.

No human community is perfect, and that includes our diverse Buddhist community in Bodh Gaya. It's tempting to spend too much time busy in our own centres, ensconced in our own comfortable, safe and secure world, food, language and culture, and neglecting to spend time around the bodhi tree. It may be a little difficult sometimes but we need to make the effort to spend time there, in contact with our deepest ideals and with other traditions and constantly reminded of the Buddha, who is central to all of us. No matter how big and important we may feel in our world, in our centre, there is a bigger community outside. This helps us to keep perspective. Perhaps after all we and our tradition are not the centre of the universe!

Buddhism in Bodh Gaya is a mixed bag, stimulated by very different motives. There are some very genuine people who really are pushing their own limits through practising the Dhamma, helping others and staying in touch with the spirit of the teachings. At the other extreme, some people – even if they are ordained monks – may have been attracted to Buddhism because of the free travel, food, medicine and accommodation. Some may have become monks because their culture expected them to do so, whether they were interested in the Dhamma or not. Some, even if they started out like that, have genuine commitment, and others are just going through the motions, or doing their best with the lot in life they have been given.

Buddhists in Bodh Gaya have a lot of friendliness and respect for each other, and usually treat each other with courtesy and affection. Sometimes the sense of unity runs deep, sometimes not. Maybe we just tolerate each other and don't really meet on a deeper level, while under the surface there may even be a degree of suspicion. It is not easy to compare the vast array of Buddhist traditions; they are so different. For example, different schools view the Buddha in different ways, from seeing him as a human being to giving him an almost magical status. But still, there are things that unify us. Sometimes it is just a matter of a difference of style that needs to be understood; we all have to work through the process of clarifying what is cultural expression and what is deeper doctrinal difference.

The variety of human beings in Bodh Gaya is breathtaking. It is full of very diverse, random, eccentric people, and also some extremely orthodox ones. Whatever the tradition in which we ourselves practise, we have to take on board others' ways of practising and living, while our own ideas and approaches, assumptions and habits are exposed and challenged. We might feel insecure and undermined or start to ask questions. Bodh Gaya is a challenging place to be and a fertile place for deepening our understanding of our commitment as Buddhists.

Sometimes we are so familiar with 'our' way of practising, and so unfamiliar with alternatives, that we immediately respond to anything new with suspicion. We may even think that 'ours' is the way to practise. People may take refuge in stereotypes: 'we are the purest', 'we are the highest', 'we are the most original', etc. The sectarian approach is limited, presenting one part of Buddhism as being the whole thing, seeing one type of Buddhism as 'the' way and all other schools as distortions or deviations from the Buddha's teachings. When we arrive in Bodh Gaya we have come from our own worlds, and ideas about ourselves and other traditions are bound to be ingrained in us. The danger is that we may keep hold of these attitudes and look at the rest of the Buddhist world in this way. Most people who come here are meeting other traditions for the first time and lots of feelings will arise when we all meet each other.

What we have here is a great opportunity to look at our attitudes to other traditions, be honest about what those feelings are and be prepared to be receptive to a different point of view. We can meet people of other traditions in a friendly way and find out about them and their lives. Within this context the old and rigid ideas can get some fresh air and maybe even some appreciation for the other traditions will arise, a softening of our views about 'us' and 'them'. Sometimes you may be aware of differences between how you practise the Dhamma and how another tradition approaches it, yet when you find yourself sitting next to someone from that tradition and start talking with them, you may find so much in common that the differences can be seen in the perspective of the broader feelings of unity and harmony. We have a choice. When confronted by other traditions, we can either reinforce our position and perpetuate our differences, or open our hearts and minds to something new. Our aim as Buddhists should be not to identify with any group or category we are conditioned to be part of. We need to recognise our fixed views and make an effort to overcome these identifications and ways of seeing ourselves. We are trying to become true individuals, free from all that weight of group conditioning. Another danger is that we may give nonessential things a central position, at the expense of things that are really more important. We can work against this tendency – whether we see it at work in ourselves or others – by emphasizing what is essential, to the best of our ability.

It seems to me that the different orthodox traditions are not just going to jump into an ecumenical approach, but will mostly keep to their own traditions. But what we are beginning to see is a softening up of the attitude that 'ours is the only way, or the best way' and an interchange of inspiration and ideas. None of us can know the effect of that over the next few hundred years. Maybe we can begin to experience ourselves as something bigger than 'our' tradition, or at least start to become less attached to our own identity. Even identifying with 'being a Buddhist' is limiting and will have to go eventually, but letting go of our tradition or tribal identity is a start. A very useful practice is to keep an eye out for conceit. All of us have to be careful that we don't fall into the trap of feeling arrogant and superior because of our tradition's approach to things. Any notion of being superior, inferior or even the same as another person arises from an obsession with the 'self'. When I'm in the temple I make sure I reflect on this every time a notion of superiority, inferiority or equality appears in my mind.

If you feel challenged by something and find yourself thinking 'That's not very Buddhist', it's a good idea to respond by asking questions. Enter into dialogue with that person or ask other people about them. You may realise that you are only at the beginning of understanding their actions and motives. It can take a very long time to come to understand someone else's motivation and the context they operate in, to know another person's world. People are all deep mysteries, not to be judged in an instant. It could turn out over time that what is happening isn't 'very Buddhist' or in line with the Dhamma. That possibility is always there in any tradition. But it is good to get to that point through metta (loving kindness), inquiry and understanding, rather than coming up with simplistic interpretations of what we think is happening, or basing our assumptions on third-hand stories. To use the language of Tantric Buddhism, to come here is to enter a cremation ground of limited views. It is to allow those views to die and open ourselves to something new.

Bodhitree Mike said: 'Some say that practising here is a bit like stepping into a pressure cooker. There is so much movement going on, with people coming and going. This place has an exceptional blessing power and also the ideal conditions to bring up whatever poisons you have inside. It is a rare combination and an exceptional context for practice. If it were only blissful and peaceful, a lot of the garbage inside you would remain there, but because it's got that other side, where other people challenge your attachment and aversion, being here *is* practice, meeting with other people from different traditions and dealing with what that brings up.'

As long as we work on understanding each other and building friendships, we can move towards a greater sense of unity. If we see Buddhism purely in terms of our own tradition, we may have a limited sense of what it truly is to be a Buddhist, but if we can see how Buddhist principles apply to other cultures, that gives us a deeper understanding of those principles. Imagine only being able to see through one eye, then having the sight restored to your other eye. You would get a much clearer and fuller sense of life. If the same applied to the eyes with which you see the Dhamma, you would be able to see it that much more clearly. And if you imagine having numerous cultures and traditions all together, as long as you concentrate on trying to see what is essential to them, rather than getting dazzled by their outer appearances, that would give you a really good view of those principles applied over and over again.

Of course we can't know how Bodh Gaya will develop, but the principle of karma makes it certain that if we act on the basis of open-minded and genuine dialogue with each other then Buddhism and Bodh Gaya will be strong, while if we reinforce our partisan attitudes, division and misunderstanding will happen. Bodh Gaya is not just about recognising our historical roots; it is just as much about the future of Buddhism. The Dhamma really does offer the nectar of liberation for those trapped in the rounds of suffering. It is not a game. The world needs a strong Buddhism, and its future is in our hands.

9

A Buddhist renaissance?

My heart swelled with emotion as I rode along the bank of the river, through groves of screw-pines and palmyra-palms, and passed pilgrims journeying afoot to this holiest shrine of Buddhism. Bodh Gaya is to the Buddhist what the Holy Sepulchre is to the Christians, Zion to the Jews and Mecca to the Mahommedans. Perhaps no other place in the world has been so venerated for so long a period by so many people. For twenty-five centuries Buddhist pilgrims have come – from Ceylon, Burma and Siam, from China, Japan and Korea, from Turkistan and Tibet, to see the holy tree and the place where the Buddha sat.

Anagarika Dharmapala describes
his first visit to Bodh Gaya in 1891

Buddhism is in danger in much of the traditionally Buddhist world. In Tibet, China, Mongolia, Russia, Vietnam, Laos and Cambodia it has been severely undermined by militant communism. In Thailand, Taiwan and Japan it is being undermined by consumerism and in Sri Lanka and Myanmar by militant nationalism. Many traditions are failing to communicate relevant messages in the fast-changing 21st century. In India and in the west, by contrast, Buddhism is growing.

Historically Buddhism has always taken new forms to adapt to different times and places; that has been one of its strengths, and it is why we have such a rich and diverse tradition. Will Buddhism adapt to the 21st century, and what will Bodh Gaya's place be in that process?

When two great rivers meet they energize and refresh each other, sharing nutrients and life, bringing new growth and nourishment. When one tradition meets another, new life is breathed into the teachings. If this happens with just two streams, imagine the potential, the great sea, of all the traditions living and practising here in Bodh Gaya!

In Bodh Gaya we are focusing on the historical Buddha and his Enlightenment, continually in touch with his life and liberation, and with what he taught. All of us here must see the significance of this, or why would we feel the need to be here? It's a chance for all Buddhists to connect with each other and open up to other traditions and the Buddha's influence at the same time, a collective refocusing and reinspiring.

The word *renaissance* means 'a revival of spirit' or 'to get new life and energy', a 'reawakening' or a 'revival', to 'rejuvenate' or 'prolong, renovate, refresh, revolution, revitalize, transform'. All those words seem appropriate to what it is happening here. Renaissance can also mean 'reborn', and perhaps we can say that the Buddha is 'reborn' into our consciousness, the old faded connection dusted off and brought into our hearts and minds afresh once again.

It could mean a fresh wave of energy and a new focus for Buddhism. It could infuse old traditions with hope for a new era. Traditions that are struggling could find new ways of being. Interactions in Bodh Gaya could bring fresh understanding, inspiration and new perspectives. This 'new life' could help those who live here, but also give something to practitioners of established traditions to take back to their home cultures.

A renaissance could find many ways of expressing itself in Bodh Gaya and worldwide, but one aspect it could bring is deeper unity in Buddhism, although this is a complex proposition. It might take a long time – perhaps one or two hundred years – for this fusion to take place, but that would be OK. If we sow the idea of a renaissance, and we work at the conditions that may give rise to it, it is more likely to happen.

We have no idea what form a revival of Buddhism in Bodh Gaya might take. A lot of conditions are in place and a new surge of people from all over the world who are committed to Buddhist ideals could have a profound effect. When I asked Bodhitree Mike, 'Will a renaissance take place here?', he said, 'It is already happening. Each one of these groups is coming from a single context and when they see others, they get a larger sense of what Buddhism is, and they look a bit more deeply at what they have taken for granted. When we see each other practising, that is inspiring. These *tripitika* chantings, where all the different traditions chant together, have a great effect on those who take part. In this holy place it takes on a new significance. It has taken a few years to get it together but now it is working and it will continue to grow.'

Most traditions do tend to focus on their internal affairs rather than on unity, but it is definitely there, and people enjoy being here for that reason. Why does a renaissance matter? As I see it, the rejuvenation of Bodh Gaya is important for the whole Buddhist tradition, and for the world as a whole.

When I asked Bhante Sewali, the head monk of the Maha Bodhi Society, whether he thinks a renaissance in Bodh Gaya will filter back to different traditions in their own countries, he said, 'Different traditions are always there because they are coming from different countries and cultures, but the culture's tradition and the Buddha's tradition are different things. The Buddha never had any tradition; he went beyond everything and was universal. When we look at a tradition in a culture, that is OK, but when we think of a universal tradition we need to think in a wider sense, without limits.'

Nalanda

One of the difficulties of guessing the effects over time of this renaissance is that there is really nothing in Buddhist history to compare it to. But we might get a clue from Nalanda. At Nalanda, which is about 90 km from Bodh Gaya, there was once a Buddhist university, one of the oldest universities in the world. It had nine million books, 2,000 teachers and 10,000 students from all over the Buddhist world. This centre of great learning flourished between the 5th and the 12th century CE.

Nalanda was a truly significant place in Buddhist history and it can give us an idea of what is possible when many traditions come together. A lot of what formed Tibetan Buddhism, both its Mahayana and Vajrayana traditions, stems from the late (9th–12th century) Nalanda teachers and traditions. The scholar Dharmakirti (7th century), one of the Buddhist founders of Indian philosophical logic and one of the primary theorists of Buddhist atomism, taught at Nalanda. Other forms of Buddhism, such as the Mahayana Buddhism practised in Vietnam, Korea, China and Japan, flourished within the walls of the ancient university. A number of scholars have associated some Mahayana texts, such as the *Surangama Sutra*, an important sutra in East Asian Buddhism, with the Buddhist tradition at Nalanda. Could Bodh Gaya be the new Nalanda? Is that spirit alight here?

When interviewing Sangharakshita for this book I reminded him that in his memoirs he said that he and Jagdish Kashyap (one of his teachers) wondered whether now that Buddhism was returning to India, it would be possible for a new Nalanda to rise from the ashes of the old. I asked him what comparisons there might be between Nalanda as it was and Bodh Gaya as it is now. He pointed out that Nalanda was focused on study, while Bodh Gaya today has a different focus, although one that includes Dhamma study. This is very true; the focus here is on the Buddha's life and Enlightenment as an object of faith and reflection, and his embodiment as a synthesis of history and myth.

In my view, Bodh Gaya is a place with great potential *because* it is based on a direct spiritual realisation which all traditions come from and relate to rather than on study. I would say that Dhamma study is always going to be tinged by partisan approaches which might have some limitations. Agreement about which texts are central cannot necessarily be found, but no one can deny the centrality of the Buddha's Enlightenment.

One word I'm exploring at the moment without any resolution yet is 'Buddhayana'. The term *yana*, which means way or vehicle, has been applied to three historical phases of Buddhism: Hinayana, Mahayana, Vajrayana. I asked Sangharakshita if the term 'Buddhayana' could be used to describe the next phase of Buddhism's development. He said: 'It is quite possible. It could be a fourth yana, or a way of unifying the other three.' If we play our part, history may even look back and see Bodh Gaya in the 20th and 21st centuries as being a truly significant time and place in Buddhist evolution. What a great opportunity for new life to emerge here, and reach out to new worlds in this century and beyond! It may take time – making friends, and developing trust, unity and openness all take time – but hopefully we will have time. After all, Nalanda was around for 700 years.

10

The challenge
of Bodh Gaya

It is to Buddha Gaya, to the Diamond Throne beneath the bodhi tree, rather than to the garden at Lumbini or the quiet grove at Kusinara, that the main stream of our devotion flows. As we sit, morning and evening, and meditate on the Buddha's Enlightenment, there dawns upon our inner eye a vision of the stately spire of the Maha Bodhi Temple as it rises above the tops of the surrounding trees. We see the great bodhi tree, lineal descendant of the one beneath whose branches the young Indian ascetic sat, five-and-twenty centuries ago, resolving that though the blood should dry up in his veins, and his body crumble to dust, he would not stir from his seat until Enlightenment had been attained. For an instant we have, as it were, a glimpse of a Figure sitting radiant and victorious in the rays of the early morning sun, and hear the songs of praise which were echoed by the deva hosts from the earth even to the highest heaven. Then the centuries roll like clouds across our mind's eye, and when they have passed we find ourselves back in the twenty-fifth century. The Eye of Faith, which opens so rarely, has closed and the eye of flesh sees Buddha Gaya as it is today …
Sangharakshita writes of Bodh Gaya in the Mahabodhi
Journal, 1954 (reprinted in *Beating the Drum*)

The safe and convenient means of transport developed over the last fifty years make it relatively easy for us to move around the world, and enable us to meet people not just through reading books or being told stories of distant lands but face to face. We live in an increasingly interconnected world, and Bodh Gaya is a microcosm of that. People from vastly different cultures and nations, the most unusual and different people you can imagine, are drawn by the pull of Bodh Gaya. It seems amazing to realise that we all have a unifying point in the Buddha! When looking around the temple or going through the market place I am instantly struck by the incredible variety of people who would never have met each other until now. Even after many years of coming to Bodh Gaya, I am still fascinated by the strange, delightful and unusual characters who walk by. If you think your own Sangha is full of eccentric people, wait until you meet the rest of the Buddhist family!

We all bring so much with us when we visit or move to Bodh Gaya. Here there are different Buddhist traditions, Dhamma teachings, communities, practices, rituals, styles of chanting, meditations and festivals. There's a rich tapestry of culture, literature, languages, celebrations, arts, aesthetic styles, temples and communities, gardens, stupas, statues, ritual instruments, customs, friendships, music, architecture, medicines, social work, education and food. There are concerns about recycling and global warming, nature, aesthetics, values, history, archaeology, and the preservation of tradition. I'm afraid we even swap illnesses with one another.

Bodh Gaya's growing popularity over the past forty years has been a mixed blessing. There are some dangers that could undermine or dilute the significance of the place, take it in another direction, or make it lose the Buddha's spirit. As the express train of Bodh Gaya gathers speed we have to make sure that it is going in the right direction.

Not everyone has been viewing its recent success with altruistic eyes. A lot of different types of people are attracted to Bodh Gaya, which is a small economically successful bubble in the vast wilderness that is the state of

Bihar. (Sometimes I think jokingly, why didn't the Buddha gain Enlightenment in the Bahamas next to some nice beaches? But Bihar has a way of making sure that people coming here have purer motives. It isn't exactly full of hedonistic attractions; it can be a challenging place to be.) A lot of people in local businesses, and in local and national government, see Bodh Gaya as no more than a massive business opportunity. In a way this is understandable. The Indian tourist board naturally has an agenda based on money and development, and local businesses will want to make the most of the situation – which is all to the good for visitors who need places to stay, food to eat and rickshaws to travel in.

The danger is that tourists and businesses may start to dictate the atmosphere of the place. There is so much distracting shopping that it can start to dominate pilgrims' time and attention, and they forget to prioritise spending time at the temple. Aggressive sellers at the temple and noisy traffic destroy some of the atmosphere too. But despite problems like these, at least the temple is alive and vibrant, not a historic monument or museum like some of the other Buddhist pilgrimage sites – Sarnath, for example.

Of course it is very good that Bodh Gaya welcomes the faithful, and tourists as well, but masses of unaware people flooding the temple can dissolve its integrity, and there could come a point where the balance will tip, and its position as a place of practice, worship and reflection could be lost. We have to work hard so that the Buddhist principle of living Sangha is the strongest presence in and around Bodh Gaya. Bodh Gaya is so important and has such potential that allowing its special atmosphere to be dissipated would be tragic.

One thing I have found difficult is that over the years I have felt less physically connected to some aspects of the temple. I feel especially sad that glass casing has been placed over the Buddha's stone feet so no one can touch them. I am an earthy type of person and very tactile; I love touching, feeling and connecting to things physically. Putting my head on glass feels a bit weird. And now the railings around the *vajrasana* have been shut, so we can't touch it or sit inside right next to the tree; that's a bit alienating too. When I first came to Bodh Gaya in 1998 there was much freer access to the temple. These problems are one of the downsides to Bodh Gaya's popularity; the temple's sacred places have been hidden for their own protection against the millions of visitors.

A friend of mine, Shashi, who is a thangka painter (thangkas are traditional paintings of Buddhas and Bodhisattvas) with a very highly developed sense of aesthetics, said: 'One danger is that they will try to make too many 'improvements' to the temple, like putting gold on the top. They've put cloth around the Buddha's body, but without cloth it is so beautiful. And they have cut down too many trees. I think they should just keep it simple and protect it the way it is.'

I am sorry to say that another atmosphere-crusher here can be the way Hindu pilgrims sometimes treat the place. They do not see the Buddha as Buddhists do, but relate to him as an avatar of Vishnu, and I'm afraid their rowdy visits, often by the bus load, can feel like a pitch invasion at a football match – though I hope that some of them do get some sense of the Buddha's true nature. Buddhists around the temple can also be unmindful and show an insensitivity and lack of regard for each other; we do need to pay attention to the basic aspects of mindfulness.

Amplified sound around the temple can destroy the atmosphere completely. The temple itself pumps out Buddhist chanting at painfully loud levels at certain times of the day. The people in the market place who sell chanting CDs play them through speakers, and some of the temples have their own speakers dotted around the village. Another noise problem around the village is created by televisions and loud music in cafes or on the street. Then there are the Muslim calls to prayer, and the local weddings, parties and celebrations, which can go on all night and often have tractors driving around with massive speakers on the back and hundreds of people dancing.

Practising tolerance is OK if things can't be changed, but there are things that can be done. The temple management committee is thinking of making a rule that there should be silence between 7 and 9 for meditation hours. I can appreciate that it is difficult to find a balance between complete freedom of action and guidelines to make sure that people are not acting too irresponsibly.

One of the questions for Bodh Gaya is how to be busy and popular and still keep the spirit of the Buddha. In the village there are forces of unity, depth and integration and also forces of disintegration and superficiality. It is in the midst of a very long and drawn out process of trying to become a world heritage site. One suggestion is to establish a zone around the temple at Bodh Gaya and move the present village outside of that zone, but it may be too late for that. An example of a Buddhist site where this has worked is Sanchi, which is a lovely quiet space with shops at some distance outside, but that plan was implemented before the site became too popular, and of course the other pilgrimage sites don't have the same level of popularity as Bodh Gaya. Another pressure on Bodh Gaya is produced by the big events held there, which can draw up to 200,000 people and last for a week or two. These put massive pressure on Bodh Gaya's infrastructure.

These are pressures that come from outside. We Bodh Gaya residents also create our own problems, for example sometimes getting so busy in our own centre or monastery that we don't have time to go to the main temple, or interact with others. Council meetings attended by the heads of all the international monasteries are becoming less regular. Some people find that language is a problem; English is the international language and we can talk to each other, but the limitations of language still cause problems. And on a practical level, some people from colder climates struggle with the weather conditions in Bodh Gaya. All the heat and dust and mosquitoes make it like a hot hell, one Tibetan lama told me.

A concern that I have is that nothing should compete for attention with the great bodhi tree and the temple, which symbolise the Buddha's Enlightenment. They should be central to Bodh Gaya, a focus for all of the Buddhist traditions to live around, like a living mandala. There could be a danger of losing this if huge inappropriate statues are built. To my way of thinking, any statue bigger than the main temple seems to be competing for attention as the focal point of Bodh Gaya, which feels wrong. We don't want Bodh Gaya to become a Buddhist Disneyworld and thus a magnet for millions of tourists. Statues are very beautiful and I do love the 80-foot-high one that is here already, but I hope that these are not just empty idols to attract tourists to take pictures. May our temples be filled with living Sangha and express the Dhamma for the benefit of all who come here!

11

Visiting
Bodh Gaya

O, let us doff the glittering brocade of superficial modern intelligence, and don the coarse red homespun garment of simple faith! With the burden of long-suffering on our backs, and with the staff of endurance in our hands, let us join these humble pilgrims from the mysterious Land of Snows and trudge with them along the long and dusty road that leads to Bodh Gaya. With the Sacred Words on our lips, with the golden flame of faith and love burning in the transparent alabaster chalice of wisdom within our hearts, and with the Blessed One Himself for our guide, let us go forth as pilgrims upon the Middle Way that will lead us, one day, even to the Heart's Enlightenment.
Sangharakshita writes of the inspiration that arose
from seeing Tibetan pilgrims arriving at
Bodh Gaya (in *Crossing the Stream*)

Bodh Gaya is a unique place, and presents visitors with challenges that we might meet for the first or only time here. In the winter season it expands like a mighty lung as thousands of pilgrims flock to this place, swelling the numbers of the 12,000 permanent residents of the village and monasteries. It is like a crazy mixture between a big rock festival, an art gallery and a shrine room. Pilgrims come in waves, sometimes to one big event, and about 2,000 practitioners stay here all winter, some of them returning every year. Bodh Gaya is at the centre of a whirlwind of people.

With air travel contributing to global warming, we all have to make an informed choice about travelling here, and it's hard to weigh up the pros and cons. I would say that a pilgrimage, especially one to the heart of Enlightenment, has a different dimension of infinitely greater value than travel for any other purpose. With regards to safety there are certainly things you need to think about when travelling in India, but if you bear these in mind there is no extra risk involved in travelling in Bihar state, especially given how many people travel to Bodh Gaya these days.

There are many different levels of arriving here. As is the case wherever we go in the world, the longer we stay the more connected we feel. Because Bodh Gaya's significance is multi-faceted and multi-layered, it takes time to tune into its various aspects – the longer the better. If you don't have much time, any time here is better than none, but I highly recommend staying as long as you possibly can. Lots of people I've met over the years have regretted not leaving enough time for their visit to Bodh Gaya. The Lonely Planet guide recommends staying for three days, which is barely enough time to take lots of pictures and go. That's OK if you're not a Buddhist and Bodh Gaya is a Buddhist blur in your whistle-stop tour of India, but if you practise the Dhamma and meet the Buddha, you will want to stay longer.

Making offerings at the temple helps one to enter into communication with the Buddha; it is an appropriate response to meeting him. One of the purposes of offerings is to acknowledge the massive gap between oneself and one's Enlightened potential, represented by the Buddha. I find that that acknowledgement emerges as reverence. I want to offer flowers, candles, incense and many other things to respect that gap, and ask the Buddha for help to realise what he realised. Making offerings also opens up receptivity to the Buddha's influence in our hearts and minds. If I don't make offerings to the Buddha I'm likely to feel emotionally cold, as if I am somehow equal to him. Sometimes If I'm too tired or the temple is too busy for long periods of meditation, I just offer flowers, which is a great practice in itself. Sangharakshita has advised his Dhamma students not to underestimate the power of simple ritual, and in my experience it is wise advice.

There are countless places all over the temple complex for sitting and silent walking, making offerings or becoming absorbed in reflection, and thousands of tiny statues, images, symbols and figures. There are the various places the Buddha's Enlightenment experience unfolded. All are rich in meaning, and each of us will make our own connections. For example, lettering on a concrete post just as you enter the temple says 'You are a holy man by your actions, not just because of your birth'. This quotation from the *Dhammapada* is loved especially by those who are trying to break free of the caste system.

Times of day make a difference too. To my mind, the evening is a lovely time to do pujas and readings from Dhamma texts here; they seem to mean more just because they are recited in this special place.

Coming to Bodh Gaya is I believe a very weighty positive karmic event, which has the potential to sow a seed deep within our being, even if we don't realise it at the time. Making the effort to come here is acting out a strong intention to meet the Buddha. There was one occasion when I thought I was about to die. I was in an aeroplane when we hit severe turbulence. We were getting thrown around and it felt as though the plane was losing control. Fear was tangible all around. But the fear that rose up in me dissolved away, and I became quite tranquil. I could see that this tranquillity came from my connection with Bodh Gaya and other positive events in my life. To come here once is powerful, but if we keep coming again and again, both as individuals and as a Buddhist movement, we establish a very deep connection with the Buddha and his Enlightenment.

Practising here is not like being in your shrine-room at home. Just being in a new environment is challenging and delightful, but you need to get used to practising in the midst of the swirl of devotion and circumambulation. In contrast to our contained, safe and silent shrine rooms, Bodh Gaya is a semi-organised chaos. I may have left the Parachute Regiment long ago, but I still often bring to mind its motto: 'Ready for anything'!

If it's really busy and you want to gather together for meditation or puja with some friends, it's a good idea to meet in the bookshop at the temple entrance. Then, pick your spot wisely. You will want to be close to the tree and have your own space, but be flexible. You may have found a good spot yesterday, but today it may be filled with hundreds of pilgrims and a man with a megaphone. Observe conditionality at play; you can only control a small part of it. Don't expect silence or get frustrated when it is noisy. There may be a lull from time to time, but it is best to expect noise and be pleasantly surprised when it is silent. Sometimes I am completely surprised by the deep silence on an evening when I thought it would be busy, and sometimes it's noisy at a time when I would have expected it to be quiet.

There are three different paths to take when circumambulating the temple. Generally the inner and outer ones are busy, but the 'middle way' is often free, and that's my favourite one. Around the temple there are seven different places where various phases of the Buddha's Enlightenment unfolded. You can go to each of them, and reflect on what happened there. One thing I love is walking in the footsteps of the Buddha. It's especially nice in February, because the warmth from the sun stays in the paths and the earth until the evening time so you can walk around barefoot.

If you are doing collective practice like chanting or a puja, engage passionately in what you are doing, and respond with kindness to any random noises around you, whatever or whoever is causing them. Try to develop a feeling of equanimity towards the noise. If it gets really noisy, sit close together, so that whatever is happening, you can stay focused on your puja or chanting. Even if it is quiet when you sit down it is best to do this because anything can happen in the next hour! If you're being drowned out, sometimes shouting is the only option. If you can overcome your initial resistance, it can be very engaging and passionate. It is very cathartic too, getting your heart, lungs and voice completely involved. Just go with the flow, whatever crazy things happen around the tree. The one thing you should definitely remember to bring with you is a sense of humour.

Night time is a great opportunity for deeper, quieter practice. I usually do my practice at night anyway, so for me it is a beautiful meeting of two worlds: night time and the bodhi tree. To stay in the temple complex overnight you need to get a pass from the temple management office, which is not far from the temple. You will be let in at around 8.30–9pm and can leave in the morning at around 4 or 5am. Don't forget mosquito nets and long clothing. A week of nights at the temple would have a powerful effect as a retreat; there is a meditative atmosphere at night even in the busy season.

There is as much diversity in the food here as there is in the spiritual practice and the people. Bodh Gaya's cafes are very laid back and generally filled with very interesting people. A lot of discussions take place, some mundane and some more profound. I have always found cafes a great way to meet new people; there's lots of time to socialise while you are all waiting for food and sitting close to one another. Bodh Gaya is an amazing place for Buddhists to meet, a great network of friendships and co-operation. I have seen some great connections and friendships made over the years, and chance meetings between like-minded people. Dhamma discussions go on everywhere: in temples, communities and restaurants. You find yourself talking about everything from cricket to the meaning of life. Sometimes people feel a bit uneasy asking questions about the Dhamma in a group on a Dhamma course, but as soon as you sit down over a chai and a plate of momos, all the deep questions and the real feelings come out.

If you want a sample of the diversity of relationships in Bodh Gaya, just spend some time looking at the posters put up around the village in cafes and public places. You will get a glimpse into all things here. One example: 'Welcome! Saturday 5pm Tara guest house. Maps, networks and synchronicity as a metaphor building bridges between science, art and Buddhism.'

One problem in Bodh Gaya is the danger of getting confused by the 'big sweet shop' of approaches to the Dhamma it offers. It is important for beginners who are just finding their way with the Dhamma to look around and experience what is on offer, but after a while of 'shopping around' I think it is best to commit yourself wholeheartedly to a path of practice. Sometimes westerners who come to Bodh Gaya move from tradition to tradition and never fully immerse themselves. The danger is that if you start to feel challenged by the Dhamma, you can just do something else and never really face the challenge. Sometimes we need commitment and resolve to stay with our practice, along with the guidance of more experienced people. It's tempting to choose only what you want to hear, but just picking a teaching you like the sound of is not necessarily the way to find out which aspect of transformation you really need to be working on. It is often the most challenging aspect of the Dhamma that brings the greatest rewards. Also, we need a good teacher to give us the teachings and practices that will work most effectively for us, and a good supportive context in which to realise that potential. It's no good collecting initiations like boy scout badges; that's just a form of spiritual materialism.

A lot of people struggle to cope with the beggars they see in the streets in Bodh Gaya (as in places all over India). It's a complex issue because as Buddhists we are practising compassion and generosity, but sometimes we think we are being compassionate and generous when we are really not. When helping others we need to try to see what their needs are in a broad context and not just do the easy and obvious thing. It is very hard to know what effect giving to a beggar has on them; you could be helping them or you could be supporting a way of life that they have become attached to and is detrimental to them. Like most local people in Bodh Gaya I think it is better to give to a charity that works in India and has experience in using the money you give to bring about real change. Of course it's also complicated trying to decide which charities to give to, because there are so many scams around. We are fortunate because through our movement we are connected with people working in India who we know we can trust. If you support a trustworthy project, you can feel satisfied that you're doing your bit and can walk through the village and feel OK about not giving to beggars. But even if you don't give money to them, you can still treat beggars as human beings, being kind to them as you would any other human being, although sometimes they are so aggressive you just have to make a beeline through the crowd and not give them any attention at all.

Bodh Gaya's different seasons have a very different feeling to them. The winter season between October and

February has the energy of the active time of year; there are thousands of visitors from all over the world, and teachings, pujas, retreats and festivals. The tented village that appears for the winter season disappears in February/ March, and the hot season – from March until July – is one of changing routines, like swapping daily activity for an afternoon sleep. In the rainy season between July and October Bodh Gaya has a feeling of reflection and quiet. The monsoon brings the refreshing rains which take the dust from the stifling air. Because you can't go anywhere very easily and the busy pilgrim season is over, there is a comforting sense of staying still, and the conditions are naturally good for a more substantial meditation practice. The whole place has a retreat-like feeling. I can see why the rainy season retreats traditional to Buddhism in this region are so popular.

12

Just sitting
in the presence
of the Buddha

*For seven days he dwelt there – his body gave him no trouble,
his eyes never closed, and he looked into his own mind. He
thought: 'Here I have found freedom', and he knew that the
longings of his heart had at last come to fulfilment.*

Ashvaghosa describes the Buddha
at Bodh Gaya (in the *Buddhacharita*)

In Bodh Gaya I have found that as well as doing active
practices – the mindfulness of breathing, say, or the six
element practice – it is vital also to give plenty of time to
receptive practices. It is good to do nothing, the practice
of no practice, just sitting soaking up the influence of the
Buddha. Being here and practising over many years, I
have come to develop a practice I call 'just sitting in the
presence of the Buddha'.

In essence it is as simple as it sounds, and saying too
much may complicate things unnecessarily. However, I will
say a few things about it just in case they might be useful.

For me, sitting down at the foot of the bodhi tree 'just
sitting in the presence of the Buddha' is like doing my
visualization practice, my sadhana. It's developing an
imaginative connection with the Buddha, opening my
heart and mind and allowing his nature and presence to

soak into me, inviting his qualities to nourish and influence me and act through me.

So how do you start? To begin with, adopt your usual comfortable meditation posture, whatever that is. Then you just sit. There is nothing to cultivate or generate; just stay in touch with a sense of being in the present moment, open to whatever arises in you. The aim is to maintain that dynamic openness. If you've noticed that you've lost it and you've started planning your shopping, just come back to the openness again.

Develop a relaxed, open state of mind. Deal with any hindrances that arise in the same way you would in any other meditation, and just keep coming back to that open and expansive and dynamic sense of joy and concentration.

Then, bring to mind the Buddha and his qualities, through an image or a 'felt presence' of him, and allow those qualities to enter your heart and mind. It is a way of making your connection with the Buddha more personal, feeling closer to him, allowing your appreciation of him to grow. Another way to think of it is that you are receiving blessing from the Buddha, often traditionally called 'empowerment'. These qualities will begin to manifest in your life as you become an open 'vessel' for the Buddha's qualities.

You just look at the tree, temple or *vajrasana* and stay open to what is there. It's hard to say more than that really. It may help to ask unanswerable questions like 'Who is the Buddha?' Stay open to his deep mystery, and try to stay relaxed with the knowledge that you won't get a rational answer. Just enjoy your response to him and his Enlightenment, explore that relationship. What are your feelings? There is an art to just experiencing ourselves in relation to the Buddha.

Stay open to your feelings about the Buddha. Can you sense his deep peace or connect in your heart with his sun-like compassion? Maybe you can sense a light, a colour or even a sound. Maybe you can taste his victory and liberation, which happened here, in this very place. Or maybe you see him as a human being walking this earth just like us, but so much more. The main thing is to be open and relaxed to whatever comes to you and rejoice in that.

A lot of people come to feel that their connection to the Buddha becomes central to their whole life, with new aspects continuing to emerge over time. The Enlightened consciousness that the Buddha dwells in might seem a world away from our thoughts and feelings, but there is a seed of its potential in us. Something deep within us yearns for that and pulls us towards it. According to a teaching called the five *niyamas* (the five kinds of conditionality), this strong attraction is the *Dhamma-niyama*, the natural law of the true nature of things. This attraction towards Enlightened consciousness will tend to be impeded by the strength of our negative habits, but as we accumulate enough positive actions, the *Dhamma-niyama* can start acting through us. This isn't a process of will; it is more like something we can experience and allow; our practice is to listen, to wait, and to be sensitive to feeling that pull, that attraction.

Bodhitree Mike is the best person to comment on sitting under the tree, as he has sat there each winter season for many years. He is an American, and I first met him in 1998 when I stayed in a room next to him at the Burmese Vihara. Wearing white robes and with his hair always up in a top knot, he sits in the same spot under the bodhi tree for hours and hours every day, soaking up the atmosphere. As he sits there he talks with anyone who wants a chat or just sits with others if they want to just sit there. He is a genuine and friendly guy, one of Bodh Gaya's beautiful characters. When I asked him about his experience, he said: 'Coming here all these years has been of inexpressibly great benefit; I cannot even begin to put it into words. The more time you spend in this place, especially with pure motivation and great aspiration, just sitting here with an open heart, the more full of wisdom you can become, with the blessing of the Buddhas and Bodhisattvas. It is an ever deepening process.'

Just sit with the Buddha and experience his paradoxes. Looking at an image may help to inspire you. But we have no idea how the Buddha will manifest to us, we just make the effort to sit in an open dimension of being.

We get inspired to practise when we see others doing so; it is a field of merit. It is hard *not* to practise when you're around the tree, and it is easy to get concentrated. You don't even have to be trying to meditate; just come and sit here and enjoy the people and the place.

Reflection here is also very fruitful. Simple words seem deeper here, for it was here that the Buddha had a deep spiritual vision of the nature of things, and we can enter into his vision of things are they really are. Bringing to mind an aspect of the Dhamma here is also an aspect of opening up to the Buddha's influence.

It is good to educate ourselves generally about lots of aspects of Buddhism, but sometimes I think that all we need is one point of reflection, one transcendental truth to reflect on, if we really allow that truth to sink in, think about it in relation to our own experience and the lives of other people. We need to see if it makes sense for us, and let it really touch and transform us. That one simple truth can enter the very depths of our being, if we allow it to flow through all of us, so that it changes us in the deepest and most fundamental way possible.

13

The Three Jewels Centre

The ideals of the Buddha, Dharma, and Sangha are known in Sanskrit as triratna, *the Three Jewels or (as the Chinese translators put it) the three most precious things. They are called this because as far as the Buddhist tradition is concerned they embody the highest values of existence – or three aspects of the one ultimate value. Relating to them makes everything else worthwhile. Everything else exists for the sake of the essence, the reality, they represent. Every Buddhist subject or practice you could possibly think of is connected with one or more of these Three Jewels.*

Sangharakshita describes the Three Jewels
(in *What is the Sangha?*)

Buddhism was born and bred in India. At the time of the Buddha, there were plenty of conditions that supported the quest for Enlightenment, plenty of fuel to keep the flame of the Dhamma alight. It only took the Buddha's spark to light the flame of peace and freedom that lit up large parts of the world. Unfortunately, the flame of Buddhism went out in India in about the 13th century CE. Before that, it had spread throughout Asia, and the forms of Buddhism that survive there to the present are based on one or more aspects of Indian Buddhism, taking on new appearances as they took shape in different cultures. In India, however, the last 600 years have been a dark age as far as Buddhism is concerned, and it almost disappeared as an organised religion here.

But in the past sixty years or so, Buddhism has started to return to its place of birth. In a number of places in India a great revolution has taken place, begun by Dr Ambedkar, who became a Buddhist in 1956, bringing millions of people from his own (previously known as 'untouchable') community with him. Sangharakshita knew Dr Ambedkar, and when the great man died only six weeks after choosing Buddhism for himself and his whole community, it was Sangharakshita, then living in India, who rallied and inspired Dr Ambedkar's grief-stricken followers to find out how to practise the Dhamma in line with Dr Ambedkar's vision. The Triratna Buddhist Community has thus been engaged for many years with this Dhamma revolution, and many of the 'new Buddhists' in India have become Triratna Order members, so that the Indian Sangha is one of the strongest aspects of our worldwide movement.

It is the history of Triratna in India that has made it possible for us to establish our centre in Bodh Gaya. I want to give a brief history of the centre, though I can only really cover my own relationship with the land and what I remember, so this is not the full story. It started when, with great foresight, Sangharakshita asked Lokamitra to find land in Bodh Gaya. Windhorse Trading provided funds, and the Karuna Trust also helped financially, as the original plans included social work. Bodhidharma and Buddhapriya took responsibility for finding and purchasing the land, Buddhapriya moving to Buddha Gaya in 1993. The next year he met Raju, who was working in a camera shop in Bodh Gaya, and they worked together trying to find land for us. They overcame many obstacles and won many battles to secure the land; at one point Buddhapriya had his life threatened and had to go to Raju's house in Gaya for safety. In 1994 Nagasen came to help and during that year the land was bought, the boundary wall was built

Bodhi tree Mike in his usual spot   Microphoned monk

The Buddha's footprints

Top Bhante Sewali, Head Monk of the Mahabodhi society

Above Different traditions sit together for a programme

Left A monk has ripped parts of all the different traditions and made robes from it

Above Colourful crowd around the Bodhi Tree

Right Nangzey Dorjee, the secretary of the Bodh Gaya Temple Management Committee

Below Nissoka giving instructions to helpers whilst constructing the second roundhouse

The two roundhouses with straw roofs on before the monsoon rains
made us realize we needed tiled ones

The temple at night

New tiled roof being painted

The relics parade with an elephant. The back of Aranyaka's kesa and sleeveless jacket can be seen in the foreground.

A temporary shrine room structure made from bamboo for the first Order convention

The community does some gardening

Above – left to right, top to bottom The Three Jewels Centre with the blue shrine/library hut in the corner • Shashi's father (on the far right) is a very good statue maker with a good reputation in Bodhgaya. He lends us the big statues he has made until they sell, so we always have lots of lovely stone figures here. This one has just been put in place. They are very, very heavy! • Mohammed and Nissoka • The 80ft Buddha statue • The new sign painted by Shashi after Sangharakshita named the land • The front half of the centre with the new sign and half the bamboo structure

A school in Palanki village where Buddhavajra and Nissoka have given talks

Top A small bamboo and cloth structure for a three-day retreat run by Subhuti for the local people

Above Community study is held three times a week

The community plays volleyball with some visiting friends.
The space is also used for badminton.

A Dhammakranti retreat leaving the temple

and a hut was put up in the corner. By January 1995 all the work had been completed. Buddhapriya came back occasionally for a few years to keep an eye on things, and during this time a neighbour farmed the land.

We sadly lost our friend Buddhapriya in 2009. He was a man who gave himself fully to what he believed in; he was committed to helping us purchase the land because he realised its significance and because he was devoted to Sangharakshita. His actions will have transforming effects far beyond his own lifetime. We owe him, and also Bodhidharma, who did so much to make the purchase of the land possible, a great debt of gratitude.

The piece of land measures about 100 metres by 50 metres – the size of an athletics track or football field. It is one kilometre away from the main temple, which is a perfect distance: far enough away to be relatively quiet yet close enough to walk to and from the centre of the village. It's an oasis of peace, nature and nourishment, away from Bodh Gaya's busyness.

In 1996 Siladitya came and started living on the land; he was its great protector and caretaker. For years he sat in a field, miles away from his family and from the rest of our Buddhist movement, protecting it for the future benefit of all, sitting firm and rock-like in his great isolation. His meditation practice is very strong, and his love of the Dhamma touches all those who know him. He carried on living here until 2009.

I've been working on developing our centre at Bodh Gaya every year since 1998. For the first six years our team – Lalitavajra, Kamalashila, Lokabandhu, Adarsha and myself – ran a winter programme for westerners in October, November and December. Unfortunately, for various independent reasons the other members of the team couldn't keep coming after 2003. I continued to come, and turned my attention to developing the land and building up the community team which I realised would be needed here for broader development in the future. I was only physically in Bodh Gaya for three months a year in the winter time, but during the rest of the year, when I was back in the UK, I worked on the many things needed to develop our centre here.

I realised that we needed people to come and live in the community and for that to happen we would need more buildings. In 2005 I presented slide shows in a number of Buddhist centres in the UK and Ireland to raise funds, and with the money I started to build a roundhouse in the corner of our land. It is about 30 foot in diameter and can sleep six, with its own veranda, kitchen and bathroom. I had a hole dug out for the septic tank, and raised money to plant trees.

I made the roundhouse out of natural materials taken from local sources; the floor and walls were made from bricks with an earth coating, the windows were made from wooden frames and glass, and the roof was made of straw. But Sachin, who was the first new community member to move in, got flooded in the monsoon, so we had to give up on the romantic idea of a posh mud hut, and laid concrete floors instead. So I had to do some more fund-raising to upgrade the floor.

In 2006 I started fund-raising for another roundhouse which would go next to the present one and be used as a guest room. It has two rooms, a veranda, a kitchen and a bathroom. I put a tiled roof on it with cirki grass as a frame. The grass acts as insulation when the weather is cold and has a cooling effect in the intense heat. In 2007 I finished the second roundhouse and plumbing system with the help of Mohamed and his family. At the time of writing (2013) we have five buildings with nine rooms at the centre, including the shrine room/library, which has two new rooms above it. Siladitya very generously paid to improve the library rooms himself. There are also the two roundhouses, and we now have a new rectangular room kindly paid for by the order convention in 2009. This room is split in two and can be used as guest rooms or as a kitchen for big events. In January 2013 we built a new toilet block, with the help of funds from the forthcoming 2013 Order convention. It's a considerable upgrade from the centre as it was when I came to live here with Siladitya in the monsoon of 1998. In those days we had one room – the present shrine room – and we did everything in that one room. We must also thank our friend Umesh, who tended the trees on the land for three years, and Santosh, who tended them for eight years. Rajender has been the gardener for two years now. The garden is delightful: simple, natural and a bit wild.

An interesting question is how we will represent ourselves architecturally. What should be our guiding principles? The temples around Bodh Gaya tend to resemble those in the home countries of those who have built them, but not having a Buddhist architectural tradition of our own, we have a blank canvas and a great opportunity to express our vision.

Our closest neighbours are the community, mainly westerners, of the Root Institute of the FPMT (the Foundation for the Preservation of the Mahayana Tradition). Our centres are about 50 metres apart, and we have a very good relationship. They use our land to put tents on if they're organising a big event, and when we have events on our land sometimes people stay at the Root, as it is very close and the accommodation and food is very good.

Community

Our community here has evolved over the years. Santosh, a mitra from a local village, lived on the land for many years. He lived with Siladitya and when Siladitya left he stayed on in the community. Sachin was here from 2006 until 2009. He was very inspired to teach the Dhamma to local people, a dynamic and outgoing person who made many friends in the local community and worked hard to develop the garden and centre. His good friend Sailesh lived here and helped Sachin for two years. Buddhavajra moved to Bodh Gaya with his family in 2009, and he is fully committed to developing the community and centre. It makes a lot of difference to have an order member here who is fully engaged in the development of the project, and can maintain the focus and depth of the community. There are nine men living in the community: Rajender, Ranjeet, Ramesh, Rajesh, Sujit, Vijay, Alok, Bali and Lalan. Buddhavajra is a good friend to them, and I support Buddhavajra and the community practically and spiritually as much as I can. I also raise funds for Buddhavajra's support and for the bills associated with the land – maintenance, gardening and so on, and I spend time communicating the vision and significance of this place. In around 2006 I was planning to start spending more time in Bodh Gaya each year, staying for the monsoon and leading a retreat here. But then Sarah got pregnant with Archie, so that plan was shelved!

The mitras in the community are mostly local men and boys who come from a number of different villages around Bodh Gaya. Buddhavajra is very good at working with them, and through them we have a strong connection with the villages they come from. Their villages are the hub of our Dhamma teaching in the area; it's easier to go into a village if we already have a connection there. The members of the community have a routine of meditation, Dhamma study, pujas and community nights. One of our biggest challenges is to set up regular financial support for them; work in Bodh Gaya is very seasonal and of course we want them to remain focused on the community and Dhamma practice without too much distraction.

Land development

I met Amitasuri, a Scottish member of our order, in 1998 on the rooftop of the Burmese vihara. We made a connection straightaway, and have met up over the years since. We both have a burning passion for Bodh Gaya. Amitasuri is one of our centre's true friends, and she is wholeheartedly supportive of the project, especially developing the land. All the work she does is despite considerable health problems; she is a great example of courage and commitment, and has brought clarity and passion to the team.

A turning point for the centre was our order convention in 2009. This was our movement's first ever gathering here in Bodh Gaya – a historic moment for the order, and for our team working on the project in Bodh Gaya. 500 order members were here, and then there was a retreat for 300 friends, mitras and order members. Sangharakshita couldn't be here physically but he graced the event in style by naming the centre via a video recording; he recorded it and had it sent to the convention, with strict instructions not to let anyone see it until the day of the naming. When he declared the name, it seemed simple yet very apt: the Three Jewels Centre. We now have a sign on the front gate with a blazing symbol of the Three Jewels, a sign that they are burning not just on the gate but in the hearts of those living and visiting here.

In 2008 a team of order members formed with the specific intention of developing the land further: myself, Amitasuri, Kumarjiv and Aryaketu. We had good times working together and had a noticeable effect here, but the team needed more input, so the format was dissolved to become part of another team. There was a lot of work to be done: setting up legal frameworks, clarifying roles, working out the steps for developing the centre. We spent two years looking at the pros and cons of purchasing more land, and had the pressure of trying to find out about Bodh Gaya's world heritage 'master plan' and its implications for us. At the beginning of 2012 a new board of Bahujan Hitay trustees chaired by Lokamitra was formed, and they want to be more actively involved. (Bahujan Hitay is the aspect of our movement in India that has initiated and developed social, medical and cultural projects in many areas of the country. Bahujan Hitay means 'for the welfare of the many'.) I am excited by the influx of new energy and keen to work together to develop our centre here. Hopes for the future include a large open-air shrine, a meditation hall, a study hall and space for up to 400 pilgrims/retreatants.

In the last five or six years Bodh Gaya has been visited by people from the Triratna community for retreats, meetings and conventions, and there is a growing realisation of Bodh Gaya's significance. It has been great seeing more and more activities here for both visitors and local people. Both Dhammakranti (a retreat for up to 4,000 people from all over India that runs every January) and NNBY (the National Network of Buddhist Youth) have taken to Bodh Gaya with a passion. Subhuti, a senior member of our Order, often runs retreats here – he has a soft spot for Bodh Gaya – and Pramodana also sponsored a retreat here. Buddhavajra and I run retreats too. An increasing number of pilgrims come and stay here when they visit. It is always a delight to have travelling pilgrims here; this is Triratna's home at Bodh Gaya and everyone should feel welcome.

The way I see it, the Three Jewels Centre is a lotus-bud waiting to flower. We need to think about what is needed here – and to unlock its potential, many things are certainly needed. Sometimes we feel the vastness of the undertaking, but the Buddha is our constant companion.

We are like a mother nurturing her child or a gardener helping a sapling to grow. We care deeply about Bodh Gaya and its potential to influence our movement and the broader Buddhist world. I think our centre at Bodh Gaya is a source of deep beauty for our movement and the whole Buddhist world, and needs to be loved and cherished. It has the potential to influence and transform our relationship with the Buddha and play a part in shaping the future of Buddhism. The centre has been evolving steadily in recent years, both in infrastructure and community, and now everything is in place for us to take the next step.

Bodh Gaya is a diverse, sophisticated, complex situation, with many levels of significance. In response to this sophisticated diversity, I feel we need to create something at the Three Jewels Centre that is deeply appropriate and sensitive to its surroundings, bringing an artistic sensibility to our collective vision of living and practising together. Whatever we create here also needs to represent our whole movement across the world so that when visitors come they get a sense of the depth and breadth of our international tradition. The various Dhamma centres in Bodh Gaya are in a way like embassies; they are a doorway into the particular expression of the Dhamma in the culture or tradition to which the centre belongs. In the Three Jewels Centre we have an opportunity to show who we are and express our values. I feel it's a chance for our movement to cooperate in an international project with the Buddha's life and Enlightenment at its heart. If we focus our efforts on developing our centre here, many other things can flow from that: a stepping stone to reach out to the people of northeast India.

We are finding that the centre at Bodh Gaya is strengthening our movement's relationship to the other places associated with the Buddha all across north-eastern India. I am hoping as well that our centre may attract those who wish to stay and work here in whatever way inspires them, for long or short periods, or run retreats here, or hold meetings. Our community is dedicated to supporting anyone who wants to work here, and to providing translation where appropriate. There is certainly plenty of scope. We very much need to establish a new generation of Dhamma teachers here, and there are all kinds of other creative possibilities, depending on the skills people have – storytelling, perhaps, or yoga teaching, or art projects. There is so much we could do. Material help is always welcome too, and we always appreciate it when our visitors manage to squeeze a book or two, or a few CDs, into their backpacks to add to our tiny library.

One very important aspect of our order from the point of view of our presence in Bodh Gaya is the strength of our movement in India. We were the first centre in Bodh Gaya to have a big event celebrating Dr Ambedkar, whose work was so crucially important for the reintroduction of Buddhism to India in the 20th century. We are a forward-looking movement, I would say, and that puts us in a good position to make the most of Bodh Gaya's significance and be able to offer something that is relevant here. In the words of Lokamitra: 'As more and more people in the west turn to Buddhism, as Buddhism continues to return to China and is reborn in India, Bodh Gaya is going to become even more significant. All this will open vast new horizons for our movement in ways we cannot imagine at present, while at same time presenting us, as individuals and as a spiritual community, with new demands and challenges. If we can make use of these opportunities, the very special coincidence between the approaches of Dr. Ambedkar and Sangharakshita stands to benefit many more people throughout the world.'

Our centre would not exist today without all those people who have created it: the people who have given and continue to give financial support (see our fundraising page at http://www.justgiving.com/bodhgayaproject if you feel inspired to do so yourself), and all those who have physically worked on it. We owe them all a great debt of gratitude, and aim to repay them by the work we do here, which their generosity has made possible.

14

The Triratna Buddhist Community

In 1949 I was in Bodh Gaya, where the Buddha had attained Enlightenment, staying at the Maha Bodhi Society's rest house. Rimpoche was staying at the nearby Tibetan gompas, of which he had recently been appointed abbot by the Tibetan government. Looking out of the window of his room one day, he espied me on the flat roof of the rest house. So astonished was he to see an Englishman in yellow monastic robes that he called out to his attendant. 'Look!' he exclaimed, 'the Dharma has gone as far as the West!'

Sangharakshita describes his first encounter with
his teacher Dhardo Rimpoche (in *Precious Teachers*)

Everything that the Three Jewels Centre can contribute to Dhamma life in Bodh Gaya is connected with the tradition we are part of: the Triratna Buddhist Community (previously FWBO, founded in 1967). Triratna was born out of a need for a new way of engaging in the spiritual life that is relevant to the contemporary context. As its founder, Sangharakshita, has explained, it has six distinctive emphases:

1) We are an ecumenical Buddhist movement

This means that we accept the whole Buddhist tradition. Not identifying with any one particular group or tradition, we learn from all, we appreciate all and we are inspired by all. In our Dhamma study we study Pali suttas, Mahayana sutras and many other texts, and our meditation practices are also taken from different parts of the Buddhist tradition. We aim to take the historical Buddha and his teachings as our central focus, and seek to connect and refer later developments in Buddhist teaching back to the teachings of the historical Buddha. We do our best to think critically and pragmatically about the kinds of Dhamma practice that best suit the conditions we live in, and to see doctrines and practices in their historical and cultural contexts, trying not to take things too literally. In short, we see ourselves as a new school of Buddhism rooted in the old ones.

I think this puts us in a good position to relate to the whole Buddhist tradition as it is represented at Bodh Gaya, and thus help to create harmony. We experience ourselves as part of a broad Buddhist context, so when I meet practitioners from other traditions here I feel that I am meeting part of 'our' tradition, rather than relating in terms of 'us' and 'them'. At the same time, we are free from the weight of orthodoxy, free to draw from the whole of the Dhamma in whatever way is needed in our context.

2) Ours is a unified movement

Our movement has centres worldwide, and men and women are ordained into our order on the same basis. Ordination is based on the effectiveness of an individual's going for refuge, and we do not exclude anybody because of their gender, their caste or their sexual orientation.

One radical feature of the Triratna Buddhist Order is sometimes expressed as 'commitment is primary, lifestyle is secondary'. Essentially this means that it is commitment to the path that is the measure of practice, not whether one is 'monastic' or 'lay'. From the point of view of monastic schools of Buddhism, which have sets of lifestyle rules to observe, this seemingly simple approach is pretty radical. But as Buddhism faces multiple challenges in the 21st century it needs to go back to its roots both literally and metaphorically and somehow reinvent itself, which is not going to be easy. For a real meeting of minds to take place, each tradition needs to take a new perspective which lies outside its existing point of view.

As I have met Buddhists of many different traditions over the years, of course I have wanted to explain the approach of my own tradition to them. I have met a lot of people who solidly adhere to their tradition's view and won't budge (and of course they may think the same of me), but I have also met many who like the idea of commitment being primary and lifestyle secondary, and even some who have been envious of that approach.

Our understanding that commitment comes first and lifestyle second is very simple, but I think it solves a lot of problems. One problem I see sometimes in Bodh Gaya is that westerners go in and out of robes, sometimes living monastically, sometimes not. I think it's the 'all or nothing' of the monastic/lay split that people struggle with. But in my own order, when we are ordained, it is one ordination for life, even if we change our lifestyle. If I want to live in a different way, I don't have to give up the spiritual life and resign from the order. Some order members do take a vow of celibacy as part of their practice, in consultation with their spiritual friends and teachers, but theirs is still the same ordination as that of people who are in relationships or living a family lifestyle. Some people in the Triratna community live in single-sex communities, and this gives us a chance to live and practise in a more focused and intense way. I lived for many years in men's communities and have found them very spiritually effective.

We don't have an official style of dress, but for meditation, pujas and other spiritual practices, order members wear a kesa round their neck to show their commitment to the Three Jewels. Although Triratna is not generally a robe-wearing order, at Bodh Gaya we often wear blue kurtas – three-quarter length shirts – and some of us wear the blue robes that we wore on our ordination retreats. I find it beautiful to see a sea of blue, or that blue shade dotted among the reds, ochres and browns of the robes of those from other traditions. These outward expressions are also a good way of recognizing other people from our movement. A number of times I have made contact with people here because they have seen my kesa or robe, or I have seen their shirt, and even though I don't know them we can instantly connect.

Most of the time I have been working here, I have worn normal clothes and a kesa when leading something. I have always felt happy being a westerner in jeans and T-shirt, but when Subhuti came here in 2009 he and Maitrivir-Nagarjuna wore blue robes. I joined in, and since then have always worn my blue ordination robes in India. Within this context I feel that this is a truthful and accurate expression of who I am. I am not a monk, and I am not a lay person. Unfortunately, no matter how many times I say that to people, it takes a very long time to dissolve the general assumption that we are lay people. We are serious, committed practitioners, and I feel that there is a gap between who we really are and how people see us. Wearing a robe is nothing special in Bodh Gaya, any more than wearing jeans and a T-shirt is, but when people see my robe, they conclude that 'He is one of us but he is different', and that does result in more respect for me as a serious practitioner of the Dhamma, and I think it helps my effectiveness here.

I think people assess you on the basis of what they see you doing over time, so exemplification is a very powerful way to have an effect. You can give a hundred talks about Buddhism, but when people see you putting it into effect in your life, exemplifying it, that can bring about tremendous faith, understanding and confidence. I am proud of the fact that the Triratna order gives equal status to men and women, and very much enjoy seeing women order members leading pujas near the bodhi tree. It really makes some monks look twice, especially if women are not ordained in their own tradition.

The sheer variety of people seen wearing the kesa shows the diversity of our order. We have centres in so many places all over the world that we have experience of trying to create unity among different countries and cultures, and this could be useful for those of other traditions who are looking for ways of adapting to our rapidly changing world.

3) The act of going for refuge to the Three Jewels is central to our understanding of Buddhist life

After his awakening the Buddha had to find ways to communicate to others, to explain what he had realised and help them realise it for themselves. This instruction to others is called the Dhamma. Dhamma is to be defined not so much as this or that particular teaching, but rather as the sum total of the means whereby Enlightenment may ultimately be attained. When asked by his aunt, Mahaprajapati Gotami, how to determine whether or not a teaching was in accordance with his vision, the Buddha is quoted as saying: 'Whatever teachings conduce to detachment and not bondage, to frugality and not covetousness, to energy and not sloth, to delight in good and not delight in evil, this is the Dhamma.' The Dhamma is a means to an end, that end being to wake up as the Buddha did when he became Enlightened. The Buddha compared his teaching to a raft – of use while crossing the water, but to be left behind when you reach the other side. We could perhaps say that the different Buddhist traditions are like a number of ships, some with blue sails, some with red, some with white, and some with yellow, all crossing the vast ocean of suffering. The Dhamma is simply that which moves us towards Enlightenment.

There are some core teachings which are the foundation of all other Buddhist teachings, and are common to all Buddhist schools and traditions. For example, there is the law of conditionality (*pratitya-samutpada* in Sanskrit), which states: 'This being, that becomes, from the arising of this, that arises; this not being, that does not become; from the ceasing of this, that ceases.' Then there are the four noble truths on which I reflected when I first came to Bodh Gaya. A third key teaching is the Eightfold Path: right view, right intention, right action, right speech, right livelihood, right effort, right mindfulness and right concentration. A majority of Buddhists also reflect on the three characteristics of conditioned existence, that all things are impermanent, insubstantial and involved in suffering.

Another central teaching is traditionally known as 'going for refuge to the Three Jewels' – the Three Jewels being the Buddha, the Dhamma and the Sangha. This is present in all traditions, although it is not always given a central place. Perhaps people would focus more on going for refuge if they realised its value as a unifying factor.

In the Triratna Buddhist Community, going for refuge is crucial to every aspect of our understanding of the Dhamma. Sangharakshita identifies five levels of going for refuge. The first is 'cultural' going for refuge. You identify yourself as a Buddhist because the group you belong to calls itself Buddhist. Perhaps you've been born into a Buddhist culture, or maybe your parents are Buddhist. The next level is 'provisional' going for refuge. At this level, you are aware of the possibility of putting the Three

Jewels at the centre of your life, and maybe under particular circumstances you do that temporarily. The third level, and in some ways the crucial one, is 'effective' going for refuge. Here you see commitment to the Three Jewels as the most important thing in life, and you are able to make that commitment. You are thus in a position to move forward towards the Buddha, Dhamma and Sangha, although if you stop making effort you slip back. The fourth level is 'real' going for refuge. This is sometimes identified with the point on the path to Enlightenment known variously as Stream-entry, Transcendental Insight, the Arising of the Bodhichitta, the Turning About in the Deepest Seat of Consciousness, the Arising of Great Faith, and so on. At this point your effort towards Enlightenment has built up such a momentum that it is irreversible. Finally there is 'absolute' going for refuge; this is the point of Buddhahood.

Not everybody who calls themselves a Buddhist is truly going for refuge; it is not signified by titles, clothes or official status. At the same time, there could be a Stream-entrant sitting next to you at the chai stall. You never know in Bodh Gaya!

When meeting each other in the Buddhist world, the important thing is to relate to one another as individuals. Even if you meet a whole collection of people in one community whose practice seems to you to be limited in some way, you may still find individuals within that community who practise much more deeply, and you may therefore be able to connect with them on that level.

Whatever our tradition, the way of the Buddhist practitioner is to approach others with love and friendliness, and speak with politeness and courtesy, in the spirit of what the Buddha called metta, loving kindness. But being polite doesn't mean giving in or suspending our critical faculty; appropriate challenge is also part of friendship and communication.

Whatever their level of going for refuge (to use that way of thinking about commitment to the Buddhist path), everybody brings something to the mix. The way I see it, each temple, vihara or Dhamma centre in Bodh Gaya is a valid expression of a style of taking refuge, each specific to its own culture and on its own level. All traditions relate to going for refuge.

From the perspective of my own tradition, I think we could find unity through seeing Buddhists in terms of their going for refuge to the Three Jewels. All traditions include going for refuge; it's just a question of realising how deeply significant it is.

I asked Subhuti, a senior member of the Triratna Buddhist Order, about finding unity, and he said, 'In my view Buddhism has to re-evaluate what the Buddha, Dhamma and Sangha are. It has to see the Buddha first and foremost in historical terms. It has to see the Dhamma in terms of the Middle Way. And it has to see the Sangha in much more radical terms, not just in terms of monks, nuns and lay people, but in terms of those who seriously commit themselves, regardless of their lifestyle. A renaissance will only happen when people begin to question their own traditions and step outside of them. What is needed is real historical critical investigation. Ideally the leaders of the traditions would lead that process.'

4) We place a strong emphasis on spiritual friendship

The importance to us of developing friendships with one another as Dhamma practitioners helps us to make connections in Bodh Gaya beyond our own circle. Although worship at the temple transcends all boundaries, it is through friendship that different worlds are understood, because it is through friendship that you can really enter the mind of another. It is friendship that shows us what Sangha is, and it is through friendship that harmony and bonds of trust can develop. In our own movement we always aim to relate to others through love and friendship; they are at the core of our tradition.

Whatever our different styles and levels of practice, there is a basic kinship and sense of brother and sisterhood between all Dhamma practitioners. We all have the Buddha in our lives, although that might mean very different things to different people. In Bodh Gaya over the years I have worked with various Triratna teams, and during that time we have made a lot of friends in other traditions. There is something powerful about witnessing each other's going for refuge over time, and this has built up confidence and trust in the kesa (the strip of fabric embroidered with the Three Jewels which members of our order wear round their necks). We are greeted with respect because there is an understanding of what the kesa means, and others have confidence in us.

Having established the Three Jewels Centre in Bodh Gaya, we have access to a great pool of collective experience, and the things we learn here can flow out into the rest of our order, enriching who we are. In the same way, the things we have created and understood can flow into and influence other traditions. Friendships are the energy of this flow. However, friendship takes time to mature in understanding, respect and trust. It doesn't happen in an instant. So we need to be patient, building our friendships with the broader Buddhist world over the years, decades and even centuries. Nalanda was not built in a day.

5) We emphasize team-based right livelihood

We have created 'right livelihood' businesses based on spiritual principles as a way of helping people to earn a living at the same time as having a fully committed and engaged spiritual life. Everyone needs food, shelter and medicine, and in traditional Buddhist countries lay people give money to support monks living in monasteries. In the west the cultural system does not support that. Some people successfully work in a regular job and integrate Buddhist principles into their work, which seems a more satisfactory approach than working in not very spiritually beneficial jobs just to earn enough money to go on retreats where the 'real' practice goes on. For people who have the right conditions to take it up, team-based right livelihood provides an excellent context for practice at work, creating intensity and providing support in the work place, so that 'work is practice' and we can engage with our practice at the same time as earning a living. As far as I can see, we at Triratna are leading the way in this kind of thinking.

6) We regard the arts as having an important place in the spiritual life

This aspect of our movement can certainly find expression in Bodh Gaya. Sangharakshita says in the volume of his memoirs called *In the Sign of the Golden Wheel* that 'Bodh Gaya (is) a centre for the dissemination of pure Buddhist religion and culture'. All Buddhist traditions are steeped in art, and we are fortunate to have such a rich heritage of meaning and transcendent beauty. But Buddhist art need not be a thing of the past. Artists of the present too are experimenting with finding ways of expressing a Buddhist sensibility through their art. In April 2012 there was a world peace arts festival in Bodh Gaya, a cultural exchange between many traditions. Sharing art here in Bodh Gaya is yet another way of connecting – with the Buddha, and with each other. I love all the musical instruments you hear and all the different images you see here; sometimes I feel like a kid in a sweetshop, surrounded by all this richness and beauty.

I am hoping that the Three Jewels Centre can be a base for arts activities. The sights, sounds, smells, taste and touch of the temple's mythical dimensions, and the way it touches the heart too, are so stimulating to the imagination. You can almost touch the Buddha's Enlightenment here, and that will surely inspire artists to come here and through their work nourish and give vision to Buddhists everywhere. Not everyone will be able to come to Bodh Gaya, but artwork created here, inspired by the Buddha and his Enlightenment, will give to those who cannot come here a sense of the magic of the place.

My feeling is that our aesthetic sense should extend to the Three Jewels Centre itself. I want it to be simple, beautiful and natural, expressing deep sensitivity to beauty and filled with nature. Over the years in different settings I have had my consciousness transformed by nature, and we can make the most of our quiet rural setting in this way. The building should be a communication in itself, and have a positive effect on anyone who enters it. The space we occupy is just as important a way of communicating our aesthetic sensibility as the things we teach.

Someone who has had a transforming effect on this aspect of our centre is Shashi Kumar, who has raised our aesthetic standards remarkably. (OK, I admit it – the place was like a tip before he inspired us to raise our standards!) Shashi made a connection with Lalitavajra when he was here, and has been a very close friend of ours ever since. He was born in 1981 in Hukhari, which is a village 40 km away from Bodh Gaya. He came to Bodh Gaya in 1995, and in 2000 he moved to Kathmandu to study thangka painting for six years at the Tsering Art School. Thangkas are elaborate, beautiful and highly detailed paintings of Buddhas and Bodhisattvas, used as practice aids in rituals and the practice of visualization meditation. By concentrating on the sacred images practitioners strive for liberation. The Tsering Art School was set up by Rabjam Rimpoche at the request of his grandfather, Dilgo Khyentse Rimpoche, and Dilgo Khyentse, as it happens, was one of Sangharakshita's eight main teachers, so there's an amazing network of connections.

A few years ago Shashi and I went to see Rabjam Rimpoche, who is the spiritual director of the Shechen Monastery in Bodh Gaya. Rabjam was aware that his grandfather was Sangharakshita's teacher, and was really interested to hear about him. I thought it was a beautiful idea that his grandfather taught Sangharakshita and I am Sangharakshita's disciple. Shashi has trained in both of our schools: in Triratna and at the Tsering school in Kathmandu. The Dhamma is like a stream. It came from Dilgo Khyentse through Sangharakshita and then me and Shashi, and it has also come through Dilgo Khyentse to Rabjam to Shashi. So the stream has joined up again. And of course the source of the Dhamma's ever-flowing stream is the Buddha.

After completing his training in Kathmandu Shashi opened the Bodhichitra thangka school here in Bodh Gaya. His vision is to re-establish thangka painting in its birthplace in Bihar, for the art originated not in Tibet but here, in the ancient Indian state then called Magadha. Shashi is the only local Indian person to have trained as a thangka painter, and now his school takes on local boys and girls and trains them in the art, and he also runs short course for pilgrims. One of Shashi's great qualities is his appreciation of aesthetics in his surroundings. Wherever he goes, beauty follows. The thangka school has great potential as an aspect of our work here in Bodh Gaya and we need to grow from that, to support our movement's vision of the place of the arts in the spiritual life.

I asked a friend of mine, Maitrivir-Nagarjuna, an Indian member of the Triratna Buddhist Order who lives in Hyderabad and is an arts lecturer, what place art can potentially take in the Buddhist world, and he said: 'Art unifies things without prejudice. It is a universal language that everyone can understand. It speaks directly to the heart and penetrates the viewer's mind. You can't explain everything through philosophy and theories. Art shows values directly. If we could produce genuine artwork from our movement, it would communicate the values we want to express, and both Buddhists and non-Buddhists could relate to it.'

It's certainly an advantage that art communicates without language, because language can sometimes be a problem in Bodh Gaya. And of course you don't have to be able to read to appreciate art, so it is a way of communicating to those who are not literate. Art speaks directly to people; it doesn't require language or education. A traditional example is the Tibetan Wheel of Life, which shows the Buddha's vision of the rounds of birth and death in images.

Maitrivir also said that 'art unifies your intellect and feelings and goes deeper', and that very much accords with Sangharakshita's reflections on the subject in his book *The Religion of Art*. Recognizing the importance of the arts to Buddhist life is one of the six distinctive emphases of our movement because at its best, art can set us free. Its process is similar to that of the spiritual life: the ego is challenged by a new way of looking at things, and the boundaries of 'self' are stretched. Of course, you need a discerning eye. A look around the 'arts and crafts' stalls at Bodh Gaya quickly reveals a great deal of not very inspiring art. Not everything that looks 'Buddhist' communicates artistic values.

Sangharakshita and Subhuti recently published a paper called *Re-imagining the Buddha* in which they say:

'To become like a Buddha we must first imagine the Buddha' and 'Unless we truly imagine the Buddha and his Enlightenment in a way that stirs us deeply, we cannot mobilise our energies to Go for Refuge to him.' I think this is connected to the need to produce works of art that allow our imagination expression. Our movement at the moment uses a lot of imagery from the traditional Buddhist world, but already order members who are artists have created their own paintings and sculptures, based on tradition but the products of their own imaginative connection with the Buddha, and their works are the focus of devotion in shrine-rooms throughout the world. It is an aspect of going to the heart of Buddhism for ourselves. In my experience, Bodh Gaya is a place that stimulates the imagination at its deepest levels. Sangharakshita has said:

> The historical Buddha is the touchstone of the whole tradition, whether as regards doctrine or imagery ... The wealth of Buddhas and Bodhisattvas that emerged in the Mahayana should all be understood as the unfolding imaginative exploration and experience of the nature of the Buddha's Enlightenment ... One Goes for Refuge to the Buddha, Dharma, and Sangha. But, historically speaking, the Buddha is the most significant of the three insofar as the other two emerge from his experience of Enlightenment: he rediscovered and made the Dharma known in this era and he formed the Sangha. The Buddha stands in the whole schema of going for refuge for the ultimate objective and content of the Dharma life. That life is lived to become like the Buddha and to see what he sees. The levels of going for refuge are then levels of connection with the Buddha. ... When one goes for refuge to the Three Jewels, there must be a felt sense of the Buddha and his Enlightenment experience within one's own imagination.

Bodh Gaya gives a profound 'felt sense' of the Buddha. This place is the original source of Buddhism, and its very earth is saturated in the Buddha's Enlightenment. Just coming here gives us a chance to touch the spirit of the Buddha and what he achieved – and perhaps to express it through our art and our imagination. Here we are uniquely placed to rediscover the Buddha. It is a place that stimulates the imagination on all levels. Here we can soak up the essence of Enlightenment and let it flow into our hearts and minds, and also into our art.

To help that happen, art and culture need to be at the heart of our centre here. We take our inspiration from Sangharakshita, who has said:

We must go back to the historical Buddha and allow his Enlightenment to express itself afresh in our own imaginations. ... The development and engagement of the imagination is one of the keys to spiritual life and should be a major aspect of the Triratna Buddhist community everywhere. We should consciously allow images of the Buddha and his Enlightenment experience to arise from our own cultural circumstances. ... All the Buddhas and Bodhisattvas who emerged [in later tradition] should be viewed as expressions of Shakyamuni's Bodhi, exploring in imaginative terms, the only ones available to us once we have reached the limits of concepts, what that Enlightenment really means. In a sense they all are Shakyamuni Buddha.

15

Buddhism in Bihar

The historical fact of the Buddha's Enlightenment beneath the Bodhi Tree at Bodh Gaya is the alpha and omega, the beginning and the end, of the entire system of Buddhism. It is the beginning inasmuch as the Dharma taught by the Buddha is not the product of mere unillumined mental activity, a philosophical system in the mundane sense of the term to be accepted or rejected at will, but a transcription into conceptual symbols of His own truly ineffable inner experience of Reality. Nor was this transcription made with the slightest intention of gratifying idle, albeit philosophically camouflaged, curiosity, but with the sole object of affording adequate practical guidance to whomsoever, possessed of faith, were desirous of treading in the footsteps of the Buddha and obtaining Enlightenment for themselves even as He had obtained it for Himself.

Sangharakshita, in an essay, 'Enlightenment', published in *Crossing the Stream*)

One of the aims of the Three Jewels Centre is to bring the Dhamma in all spiritual, cultural and artistic ways back to its roots in the local Bihari people. After all, it was in this part of India that the Buddha himself lived and taught. As Buddhism gathers momentum in India, it is all the more tragic that the people who live around Bodh Gaya have lost touch with the Buddha's vision. The irony is that many people here are born physically close to Bodh Gaya but they themselves are not close to the Buddha at all. Any sense of what he taught and who he was has been lost through the ages – until now.

In this very poor region of India, the needs of the Bihari people are complex, and there are hundreds of social and welfare projects run by Buddhist traditions and local charities in and around the area. But although there are dozens of monasteries in Bodh Gaya and they put a lot of emphasis on social work, none of them have really tackled communicating the Buddha, Dhamma and Sangha to local people. A few traditions do offer some Dhamma teaching for the locals but their approach can be too removed from local culture to be effective or too focused on attracting people to become 'good lay people'. Our movement's deep connection with Dr Ambedkar helps us to make a link with the Bihari people, and many of them have heard of him – he was after all the pre-eminent lawyer to whom was entrusted the task of drawing up the first constitution of independent India. Dr Ambedkar lit the flame which could re-ignite the Dhamma in the heart of Bihar, the place of its origin.

The Buddha said that the Dhamma has one taste: the taste of freedom. Freedom is a beautiful gift which empowers people who feel oppressed, whether by poverty or by caste, to develop confidence and belief in their own potential. To help people develop in this way, we run meditation classes, retreats, Dhamma study classes, pujas and English classes, and give talks in local villages. Buddhavajra, being an Indian order member, is very effective in working to further the local Dhamma revolution. Bihar is known for its arts and culture, so when we go to local villages and run retreats, the cultural programme we include is not just an 'add on' or something to keep the children occupied, but an important way of communicating the Dhamma.

The village talks are a highlight of my life. Seven or eight of us jump into a vehicle and head off to a village, where the local community flock around us, usually around 120 to 180 people. I talk about the Buddha and then Buddhavajra says something about Dr Ambedkar. We make a good team. After the talks some of our community do some singing, and if there is a school in the village we give out stationery. The children are adorable. One day our vehicle got stuck before it got to the village we were heading for, so I walked the last mile. I arrived in the village with a couple of dozen kids holding my hands and singing after me: 'Namaste ... Jai Bhim ... Namo Buddhaya Sadhu' – then back to 'Namaste' again. Because the younger kids can't sit through the talks, a couple of our team act as children's entertainers. We play 'Buddhist' games with them – that is, games with cultural, Dhammic and educational elements – which allows the adults to focus more on the talks and also helps communicate our vision through storytelling, games and entertainment.

Triratna's connection with Dr Ambedkar's Dhamma revolution, and our understanding that it is possible to take refuge within a family context, makes our message accessible to the villagers, I think. Certainly they always want more contact with us; we are just limited by people' and funding.

I like to remind local people to remember their ancestry. In this area the Buddha lived and taught, and some of their remote ancestors in those days must surely have been among the Buddha's followers. The name Bihar itself is derived from the Sanskrit and Pali word *vihara*, which means monastery. I want to encourage them to act on their inheritance through taking up Dhamma practice, and restore Bihar as the spiritual homeland of the Buddha's presence.

The Buddha's Enlightenment blessed this place and the power of his realisation saturates the earth itself. It is in the trees, in the air. Bihar is where the Buddha lived and walked. Bodh Gaya is where he gained liberation – here, in this very place. The earth and the trees remember him, and that memory can be tapped into today.

And if the earth of this district is saturated with the Buddha's realisation, so are the people. They have the potential – as we all do – to awaken, as the Buddha did. Bihar has had a very bad press in the past fifty years and has gained a reputation for corruption and crime, but it is full of potential. It is my heart's wish that that potential may be fulfilled. Whatever our everyday problems and concerns, those of us who live in this area – and perhaps especially those who were born here – can open our minds to the great peace and beauty around us.

Recently a monk called Jambudeep came to the centre; he lives in Bodh Gaya and reaches out to local people through cultural activities and talks, with the help of half a dozen people who support him in what he is doing. Their approach is very colourful, a mixture of fun, Dhamma and culture. They work with the Manjhi people, who form one of the lowest social groups in Bihar. Their community gained national fame in the 20th century through the extraordinary feat of a man called Dashrath Manjhi. After his wife died for lack of medical treatment because the nearest doctor was 70 km away from their village in Bihar, Dashrath was determined that no one else should suffer the same fate. Amazingly, he worked on his own day and night for 22 years to dig a road through the mountains which is now an invaluable short cut.

I went with Jambudeep to a cultural event that he had organised for local Buddhists in Bodh Gaya. There were 200 people there and when Buddhavajra and I turned up to watch, we were asked to give Dhamma talks, so with a few minutes' notice we were up on stage. We talked for about forty minutes and then the magic show started. Jambudeep insisted that Buddhavajra and I should stay on stage so the magician could do his tricks on us. After that our community sang and got the crowd singing too. My parachute regiment motto, 'Ready for anything', again came in handy! Since then some members of the Manjhi community have been on a retreat in the Triratna centre at Nagpur, so they could get a better sense of our broader movement.

16

The benefits of being
in Bodh Gaya

The great tower of the ancient Gupta-period temple, rather mysteriously situated in its hollow, gradually impresses those who approach it. As I drew near for the first time my general impression was of rather battered old age, an impression confirmed as I circumambulated the temple and noticed its shabbiness – with many of the images in the outside niches headless or otherwise damaged. Even in that condition, which was due to various British officials including an army general in the 1880s, it was extraordinarily impressive. Perhaps Buddhists should dedicate some merit out of gratitude to General Cunningham and Mr J.D. Beglar whenever they visit this temple of the Great Awakening, for without their inspired efforts, we would today have nothing but a heap of bricks. That they did this with public moneys cause them to be criticized in the Westminster Parliament for restoring 'a seat of idolatry'. On the whole they did a fine job with the resources then available. They could hardly envisage that Buddhists from all over the world would soon visit the restored temple and would later build around it temples from their own countries' traditions. Still less could they foresee that in India, where the word 'Buddha' had been a faint echo for centuries, there would arise new followers of the Awakened One who would journey there and make offerings of flowers, incense and lights.

.Khantipalo reflects on his first visit to
Bodh Gaya in 1960 (in *Noble Friendship*)

Of course, above all, being here is a wonderful opportunity for us to engage with the Buddha's life and

111

Enlightenment. When I asked Sangharakshita about this, he said that 'being here will give us the opportunity to learn more about the life of the historical Buddha and reflect on it, and also engage in discussion with other Buddhists, and practise as much as we can'. A current topic of reflection in the Triratna Buddhist Order is the importance of connecting with the historical Buddha, and being in this place which is so closely associated with him gives us the chance to communicate that connection to others who want to know more about the Buddha. For those who do know about him, coming to Bodh Gaya injects vitality and meaning into all the stories, teachings and sayings. Old teachings take on a new life here; we can really imagine the Buddha and his liberation, and our hearts are ignited with faith.

Bodh Gaya helps us develop the confidence that we *can* become Buddhas, we really can have confidence in achieving the goal. Even though we are Buddhists, on some deep level we may still not believe that we ourselves can become Enlightened. Bodh Gaya can help us to see that what the Buddha achieved we too can achieve.

I asked Bodhitree Mike about this and he said: 'Faith is based on confidence and on seeing with your own eyes that this is the right way. Faith arises especially when you see somebody who embodies the fruit of the path. You may or may not have faith in the Buddhas and Bodhisattvas – sometimes they can seem distant or obscure – but here there is a tree and a temple, very tangible objects, and you can see that here, this very place, is where the Buddha gained Enlightenment.'

One of the challenges of being here is living all the time with your highest ideals. Sometimes I'm ashamed at my reactions to things, and see how painfully far I am from how the Buddha acted, but it is only through constant contact with that ideal that we can evolve towards it.

Subhuti told me: 'In Bodh Gaya I feel how much I am not Enlightened, experiencing the gap between me and the Buddha.' I also feel that gap. When I bow to the Buddha it gives me a happy sense of knowing my place, and my relationship to the Buddha. If I thought that who I am now is the sum total of my possible achievement as a human being, this world would be a terribly disappointing place!

Looking at things from a Mahayana Buddhist point of view, Bodh Gaya can help to bring about the arising of the *bodhicitta* (usually translated as 'the will to Enlightenment'). Bodhitree Mike commented: 'Any sacred object is a focal point through which we direct our dualistic devotion to focus our attention. It creates the conditions to a point where we realise our true nature beyond our sense of separate self. If you sit here with an open heart and mind, you let go of that sense of separateness, so that wisdom can meet your heart and mind. It is so important, this place. Most people I talk to say that something inside them is touched, and I think that it's their own nature which they've lost sight of. Just sitting here it is so natural, so peaceful, so comfortable. People think, why can't I be this way all the time, and it wakes something up inside. That is the esoteric side of pilgrimage: you go to a holy place so you can connect with yourself.'

Whenever I meet people from other traditions it helps me not just to understand their tradition better but also to re-evaluate my own tradition, and thus go deeper in my practice. I thank all people from every tradition here in Bodh Gaya for helping me to do that. Bodh Gaya gives us the opportunity to feel directly part of something bigger.

In the Triratna community we take our pujas and practices from many different parts of the Buddhist tradition, so when I go to the temple, I feel quite at home. Listening to the chanting or the teaching, I can often recognize and relate to it, whether it is Pali, Sanskrit,

English, or the chanting of mantras. Something else I've noticed when staying on our land in Bodh Gaya is that anyone from our movement who spends any time here gets the chance to meet people from all over the world. You don't have to travel round the world to meet different aspects of the movement; here in Bodh Gaya there are always people visiting and passing through.

Deepening our movement

The more connections our movement has here, the more the Buddha's Enlightenment will be part of us, bringing the order into the heart of Enlightenment and the heart of Enlightenment into the order. Individually our practice deepens, and collectively our tradition gets a new perspective, vitality and faith. Bodh Gaya taps directly into the dimension of myth and transcendence that is at the heart of Buddhism.

A central myth to my life is that of service. I love the sense that I am a little bit like the 'Buddha's Secretary' here, serving the Buddha at the foot of the bodhi tree. I am always at my happiest when engaged in this life of service in whatever way is needed. At the Three Jewels Centre our aim is just to provide whatever people need to spend time with the Buddha. Serving both the Sangha and the Buddha, we provide a place to stay, a space to live in and friendship and support in any way that is needed. Ultimately people come here to spend time with the Buddha, and our aim is to help make that time meaningful and effective.

I am hoping that over time order members will see Bodh Gaya as a good place to come and discuss decisions or promote harmony in the Sangha. It is a neutral place to meet, away from your local situation, and if you are experiencing any disharmony or problems, it can help to be met here by this very powerful transcending force which reminds us of our ideals and to become less attached to our limiting views. Experiencing ourselves in relationship with our ideals, and as being part of one big and diverse tradition of Buddhism, our identity expands. And even if there is no disharmony, the Buddha's influence has a strong effect on the people who come, like an extra 'person' or force or energy giving guidance and inspiration both in and outside meetings.

Sometimes I sit under the bodhi tree thinking about a problem and it just dissolves, or I quickly gain perspective on it, sometimes without any rational explanation. The Buddha is my *kalyana mitra*, my spiritual friend, here in Bodh Gaya. So many times, through the ups and downs of creating the centre, I have sat by the tree and asked for strength, patience, compassion or wisdom. The memory of the Buddha's Enlightenment can be touched upon and breathed in. Ill will drops away and inspiration flows. It's a chance to spend time with the Buddha, the *maha kalyana mitra*, the greatest of spiritual friends.

When we open ourselves up to this open dimension of being, all the qualities of the Buddhas and Bodhisattvas rain down on us; we just need to keep inviting them in. In Bodh Gaya, words burn with deeper meaning and truth. That seems especially true of ceremonies here – mitra ceremonies, ordinations and re-commitments. We are connecting deeply with the Buddha as we take refuge. Becoming a mitra (friend) is our way in the Triratna community of declaring one's commitment to the Buddhist life. Mitra ceremonies anywhere in the world are always delightful, and they help those of us present who have already taken that step to reconnect with the time when we ourselves made that commitment, in the same way and in the same spirit, offering three simple offerings that resonate with meaning and joy (a flower, to symbolise impermanence, a candle, to represent the light of the Dhamma, and a stick of incense, to stand for the spreading fragrance of the spiritual life). Bodh Gaya lends itself perfectly to mitra ceremonies, and quite a few people have become mitras here as part of their visit. It is another great chance for all those present – both those taking part and those witnessing the ceremony – to create a strong and personal bond with the Buddha and his Enlightenment. If you meet them again, people very often tell you very proudly where they became a mitra or attended a ceremony; they love to tell the story and revel in their memories. For the same reasons, it would be a wonderful place to hold ordination ceremonies, and we have already gathered here for our order convention.

Once you've been to Bodh Gaya, it is very easy to imagine the Buddha when you get home. When I am in the UK and I chant the Buddha's mantra I am instantly transported to the foot of the bodhi tree, with all the feelings, inspirations and tangible sense of being here. It's as though I've taken a piece home with me in my heart.

You can sit under the tree and invite the Buddha to act through you, or collectively connect with the Buddha, and his influence will permeate the Sangha. Having a relationship with the life and liberation of the Buddha will deepen our movement but also being in a context where we relate to the whole Buddhist world will deepen who we are. We can draw depth and meaning from others through living and practising together. It's a wonderful experience to chant *om mani padme hum* together at order conventions, hundreds of us chanting together; imagine doing that with many other Buddhists from other traditions in Bodh Gaya! Chanting together breaks down our sense of separation and takes us deeper, both individually and collectively.

Sharing who we are

We live here among other Buddhist traditions, a body of collective experience, and our movement's increased presence here will open a doorway into a rich world of Bodh Gaya's meaning. It is a two-way flow. We can draw from this deep pool if we let the Buddha's influence and the influence of friendships and inspiration from other traditions enter our movement. And our influence can flow into this pool of collective experience, sharing who we are, and our approach and vision, to participate in the great gathering that is Bodh Gaya.

One contribution we can make is to challenge orthodoxy. Just being who we are is challenging enough for some. I feel that it is our duty to show other traditions that a new wave of Buddhism is possible. A monk once said to me that Buddhism's future is in the west. The sun is setting in the east, he said, and rising in the west. I can see what he meant, but I think that Bodh Gaya gives us a chance to change that story.

At the heart of life in Bodh Gaya there must be a living spiritual community, who live in accordance with and represent their ideals. With a strong community we can touch the lives of others, and help those who come here to see the Buddha's true nature, and become inspired by his vision. If you visit Bodh Gaya without any sense of where you are or why it is important, you're likely to just take a few pictures to upload to another blurred day on your wacky Indian website.

A vibrant Sangha must live here: not just big heartless buildings and empty shrines with only symbolic value and a market place, but a real spiritual community, helping all visitors to connect with the true significance of the place. I would rather have a bamboo shack with a plastic roof that resounded with the thunderous roll of the drum of the Dhamma than a golden palatial temple that sat silent and empty of heart.

Faith arises upon seeing the Buddha clearly, seeing who he is in his fullness, and what he taught. You cannot have faith in the Buddha without that. In *The Survey of Buddhism* Sangharakshita says, 'So long as we do not possess a clear or correct understanding of the Buddha we shall have faith not in the Buddha but in something else to which the appellation 'the Buddha' has been attached.'

The gravitational pull of conditions and cultures must not be allowed to swamp the Buddha's victory, and we must work vigorously both internally and externally against that. We need to speak up for the Buddha's vision, to be protectors of the faith, so that the flame does not go out while we are holding it. The Buddha has no human body and we must let his nature enter into our hearts and minds so that we can do his work for him. It is our responsibility as Buddhists in this era of history to sustain a Sangha here and serve all those who come to Bodh Gaya looking for the Buddha. So many people make the effort to travel here, whether as beginners who come for the first time or veteran practitioners with new and deeper questions.

Bhante Sewali from the Maha Bodhi Society said: 'Yes, Bodh Gaya is a very special place in the world. But what the Buddha realised here is one thing; his message is another. The most important thing is the Buddha's teaching. The people who come here must learn what the Buddha taught; otherwise, they will not truly meet the Buddha.' So it is our duty to practise the Dhamma here and offer it to others. Bodh Gaya is an amazing place to teach people the Dhamma. Another dimension is added to whatever is being said just because of where we are. Sangharakshita summed it by reminding me of the words of his teacher Dhardo Rimpoche: 'Live united, cherish the doctrine, radiate love'.

Gratitude

Over the years I have seen countless people from our movement come to Bodh Gaya with doubts and questions and leave with a renewed appreciation of our approach. When we are here, we get a chance to connect with the Buddha who is at the heart of our tradition, and appreciate the circumstances that brought us here.

It is traditional in Buddhism to express gratitude to your teacher, but this is no formality. We owe the person or people who taught us the Dhamma a great debt of gratitude. Despite all the diversity of Dhamma practice in Bodh Gaya, the longer I keep coming here, the more grateful I am for the particular context in which I practise, and for the confidence it gives me. The more I appreciate the Buddha, the more grateful I am to the person who introduced him to me. Whilst here I can feel the pressures of the orthodox Buddhist traditions all around us. I can sense their authority and their expectations of what the 'right' thing to do is, as though they are powerful forces that cannot be changed or diverted. My own teacher, Sangharakshita, who lived and practised in India for twenty years, could have just stayed here as a 'good monk' and pottered around doing the 'right thing', not upsetting anyone or doing anything rash. But instead he tried to work out for himself what the essence of the Dhamma was, and found a way to make it directly relevant to our culture and lives. If he had not clarified things for me, I think I would never have managed to see the essence of Buddhism, but only a mass of confusing dogma. I have deep love and respect for my teacher as a profoundly radical and open-minded person, yet one whose teaching is entirely in line with the Buddha's vision. He showed me that the truth need not be hidden in monuments or trapped in the rhetoric of old traditions, but can be alive and relevant in the 21st century.

17

The Bodh Gaya effect: the reflections of some teachers

With Faith and Energy for hands, and Mindfulness for spade,
The soil of Meditation's glade we dig deep for our bodhi tree.
Sangharakshita, 'Planting the bodhi tree',
Complete Poems

Sangharakshita has talked a number of times about Buddhism's need to return to its roots. When I interviewed him for this book he said, 'I hope the traditions that are represented at Bodh Gaya do go back to the roots of Buddhism. Some perhaps have strayed a long way from those roots, but being there might make them more aware of the historical Buddha and the Pali scriptures. We should learn more about the life of the historical Buddha and reflect on it, and also engage in discussion with other Buddhists, and practise as much as we can there.' But is this happening in Bodh Gaya in the 21st century? I put this question, among others, to a number of people with experience of living and practising the Dhamma in Bodh Gaya:

What effect does the bodhi tree have on your life here?

The Karmapa said: 'Having the bodhi tree here is a unifying factor for us. We might have separate traditions and practices, but Bodh Gaya is a place that dissolves boundaries. Here we are one.'

Bhante Sewali said: 'The bodhi tree is a symbol of the Buddha, so when we are sitting next to the tree we think of his teaching. Sitting with the Buddha gives us strength and courage, and wisdom just like the Buddha. This place is a symbol of unification without any kind of created religion. That is why the bodhi tree is so important.'

Nangzey Dorjee said: 'The bodhi tree very much helps unification because all the different cultures from different geographical areas have come to the same place. It helps to get to know each other. We see how others do the same things but in different ways, according to their own environments and culture. All the different schools do different chanting, but that doesn't matter because the meaning of what they are saying is all the same. It is a great unity and diversity.'

Do you think the conditions in Bodh Gaya will create more unity and harmony?

Sangharakshita said: 'Given the nature of the Buddha's teachings it would be very strange if there was not harmony amongst his followers, especially when we are gathered together in Bodh Gaya.'

Subhuti said: 'There is somewhere at the centre of it all, maybe beyond all of our positions, a meeting point, whether we are looking in that direction or not.'

Bodhitree Mike said: 'This temple complex is creating harmony between the different Buddhist traditions. The underlying intention for coming to this place is to transform our minds, and the more we transform our minds, the more tolerance there is wherever we are. People who come here and have been affected by Bodh Gaya can affect more people when they go back to where they live. We need to be spacious and tolerant and have a very deep appreciation of what this place represents, and then maybe our actions will be in harmony with the intent of this place.'

Bhante Sewali said: 'It is not easy to make unity of different traditions. As long as people don't realise the Dhamma they want to be separate; when they realise the Dhamma they become naturally unified. Dhamma will help us to find unity, so everyone should be encouraged to practise the Dhamma in day to day life. This is the only way to find unity. Otherwise, people identify strongly with their own tradition; this is one of the hindrances for Buddhism. If you encourage people to practise the Dhamma and discover self then we will naturally come together. All of the Dhammas are like rivers and will lead us to the ocean. The salt in the ocean is universal truth. We all come at the truth from different ways, and when we come to the truth, all of our attachment to path and discrimination dissolves. So practising together is the only way. The Buddha never divided this tradition from that one; he just showed us the path to happiness and wisdom, without any discrimination. All of the yanas came afterwards; they are nothing to do with the Buddha's teaching but a product of people after that.'

Do you learn from other traditions here outside your own?

Keiren Lama said: 'It is wonderful getting to know each other's customs and we get an exchange.'

Tenzin Lama said: 'We understand each other's teachings. In Tibet we only know Tibetan Buddhism; here we share our practice with others, and it is good for us. We practise our way and others practise theirs. There are many ways. Sometimes we go to Theravada sutras (which are teachings from other traditions). We study the philosophy of the Theravada way, and the walking meditation practised by the Thai bhiksus. When people come here they can see what is a good way for them. You can take many ideas from different traditions. Buddhism is about turning the mind; you can learn many things.'

How do we develop harmony here?

Bodhitree Mike said: 'All traditions are coming together for the first time, and you can see over the years there has been a change. In the beginning there was a lot of 'us' and 'them', which is quite surprising but understandable because everyone is coming from their country and doing things in a certain way. Now there seems to be a greater unity and harmony between the different traditions and groups that come. That is really important in this world at this time. There is a great need for Buddhism to come together, mutually respecting each other's tradition and recognizing the underlying harmony. Otherwise, what is the point of transforming our minds? If we can't develop tolerance and sympathy towards fellow practitioners, what about other people in the broader world? It is a central basic principle. Sometimes we see things in terms of conflict between traditions, but it is just one set of mental poisons coming up against another. If each of us truly embodied the teachings of our tradition, that wouldn't happen. We would get to a point beyond that so that there is harmony. Disharmony is based on ignorance, pride and jealousy. There are some here who have a great intention and others whose motivation is unclear, but they are still here and this place is still having an effect on their minds. If it wasn't for this, who knows where they'd be?'

Will the more orthodox traditions be changed at all by the experience of 21st-century Bodh Gaya?

Bodhitree Mike said: 'There have been many people who have been disillusioned by their own tradition and need some help with the underlying basis, presented in another way so that they can hear the teachings in a fresh way, but some people need to hang on to the tradition they have – that is their mind-set. But there is a need for the Dhamma to evolve in response to the times and conditions.'

Tenzin Lama said: 'I don't think they will be changed a great deal, they are *very* traditional. Westerners are much more open to new things. But it could be that abbots of other traditions will go back to their respective countries and say: "Buddhists of other traditions are just as dedicated as we are, they are just as committed, they are showing as much love and compassion and wisdom. They have different ideas about the Vinaya from us, but there is something deeper than that." It won't be instant but it does have some effect, and I think that is one of the reasons people come to Bodh Gaya. If it was fractious, tense and taut, people wouldn't want to come here, because they want a good atmosphere. So there is already a good groundswell of mutual support and unity.'

All the people I talked to expressed the need to go beyond our cultural limitations and get back to our Buddhist roots. In Bodh Gaya we are all away from our home context, and those practising in orthodox traditions can act in a slightly more unorthodox way to adapt to the context of Bodh Gaya's international nature. This is true for all of us; we all carry our cultural conditioning with us, whether or not it is that of an orthodox Buddhist tradition. But here, all of that becomes less essential than the central nature of being Buddhist. Bodh Gaya gives us a chance to focus our minds both individually and collectively on what is deepest and most central to us as Buddhists. Back to our roots – our bodhi tree roots!

Bodh Gaya is not a magic solution to disharmony, but it is a fantastic context for communication. One benefit we might get from this meeting of worlds might be a rejuvenation of our own lives and practice. Perhaps we will develop even more faith and confidence in our tradition, or find a different way of acting within our tradition. We may also get a more honest and realistic sense of the difficulties within our tradition, and be inspired to resolve these problems and create something better.

18

Glimpses
and Reflections

Ignorance was banished and true knowledge arose, darkness was banished and light arose, as happens in one who abides diligent, ardent and resolute.

The Buddha describes his Enlightenment
(*Bhayabherava Sutta*)

Imagining the Buddha surrounded by the forces of Mara gives me confidence. He wasn't born a Buddha; he battled hard for what he achieved, just as I too battle in my daily struggle to evolve.

❧

In our normal lives there is a powerful stream of samsara, and we must make tremendous effort to swim across the internal and external stream. At Bodh Gaya it is different. Here we can enter the stream of practice and go with the flow of that intensity. It has acquired collective merit over the years and today there is still intensive practice here. The stream is so strong that you almost have to go out of your way to fight against it.

Doing puja frees me from the duality which keeps me back from realising my Buddha nature.

Some people respond directly with faith. It is not studying the Dhamma that moves them, but simply meeting the Buddha.

But who is the Buddha? The more I come here, the more I will come to know him – that's what I thought, but para-doxically, he has grown in my mind, and I realise how little I really know of him. Sometimes I get a glimpse of a tiny bit of his wisdom, like seeing just the toe of a statue.

The Buddha's qualities are mysterious and very profound. Each time I come to Bodh Gaya, his qualities become clearer to me, but his nature becomes a deeper mystery. My sense of the Buddha is changing. Each time, his timeless qualities grow, and in relation to them I am getting smaller and smaller. Looking back, the idea of the Buddha I had many years ago now seems very small, so I can assume that my idea now will be outgrown in the future. To really know a Buddha I am going to have to wait until I am one.

In our spiritual journeys we are sometimes moved by the Sangha, sometimes by the Dhamma and sometimes by the Buddha. Our relationship with the Three Jewels is an ever-evolving and dynamic process. As we deepen our connections to the Three Jewels they unfold to us, bringing deeper and clearer visions of who we are. Things we never expected emerge, releasing our hidden depths and potential. The Three Jewels are alive with freedom.

Christopher Titmuss said: 'Bodh Gaya is the creative pulse that has created a long-standing and very diverse tradition. The realisation that led to all of the teachings came from under that tree, and for most Buddhists it's a life's dream to come to that spot. It is like the big bang of the Dhamma world.'

Shashi said: 'The bodhi tree has enormous energy, it is a teaching in itself. It makes people wonder why it feels different here. If you go to the Taj Mahal, it doesn't feel the same.'

I've had the experience of entering a shrine-room in England and having a strong sense of the 40 years of meditation and practice that have gone on in it. But at Bodh Gaya there is a sense of thousands of years of practice!

The temple and tree are at the centre of a mandala of myths and colours. They are radiant and pure in nature, and all things come from them. Making offerings we enter into the heart of the mandala of Enlightenment.

We see a stream of colours and dress, circling and swirling around the tree. If you put them all together, they make white light. White light is the unification of all colours, and refracts into all colours, just as when sunlight hits a crystal it creates a rainbow.

In a meaningless frantic world, this is an island of peace and meaning. Here, no longer do the fierce rivers of samsara drag me away from my purpose; here, purpose is stronger than the raging torrent. Nirvana is not a dream but a living promise that devotees long to fulfil. I too have made that promise, and it is here that I am reminded of it most vividly.

Symbols touch a deeper truth. They communicate directly to us and speak to us when words cannot express the sublime truths they embody.

Sometimes I just wander around the temple and sit in a particular spot for some intuitive reason, just a hunch. And sitting there, I see new aspects of the truth for the first time or get a new appreciation or deeper understanding of an aspect I thought I knew.

When I need to have a connection with the Buddha, I bring to mind the temple and bodhi tree, and in my imagination I am instantly connected to that felt sense of the Buddha and his Enlightenment.

Bodhitree Mike said: 'You take a part of this place with you so that when you get home you still have it with you. In taking a part of it, you become part of it. The more it becomes part of your entire being, influencing your life, the more you embody its qualities. That is why this place is so important.'

Making flower offerings invokes powers from the heart of the mandala. May I realise just a tiny glimpse of your fullness. May the blessings of the Buddhas and Bodhisattvas rain down on me. May I know your wisdom and compassion.

Buddha, what is in your heart and mind? What is at the centre of this mandala of myth, what is at the heart of your mystery? Where are you, and what is your essence?

Forgive the pious arrogance that sometimes saturates the air here. Did you mean a religion to come out of your example?

All clinging to rites and rituals as ends in themselves could be broken by a Buddha's appearance in the 21st century. There is no point in hoping that that will somehow just happen. It is up to me to practise fully and deeply. I must set my heart on Buddhahood and accept nothing less.

The Buddha is not a god. He embodies and exemplifies an ideal, and we aspire to it. He is much more than just a god, he transcends the notion of God.

Bodhitree Mike said: 'The Vajra seat is the place of Enlightenment, a place of indestructible wisdom. On an outer level it is right here in Bodh Gaya, and on an inner level it is here in our hearts.'

Sometimes as Buddhists we forget the basics: that Enlightenment is our goal, and it is we who must achieve it.

I feel fearless here. My usual doubts and sadness are dispelled, and I get a sense that if I just serve here and die here, I will create an unbreakable bond with the Buddha's Victory.

Watching colourful people carrying candles, incense, silk scarves, and a multitude of gifts and offerings, one can imagine that it is like stepping into a sutra. Some days you think 'Was that a dream, or did it just happen to me?'

Going to the temple makes me feel that I am living in a magical, mythical space, much more attuned to beauty and higher states of consciousness. I feel more content and less likely to indulge in hedonism, because I have a sense of real satisfaction and nourishment. I think we all want a deeper sense of meaning and context. Here that context is the temple, whose beauty stimulates the imagination, and produces layer upon layer of deep contentment.

When placing flowers on the earth of the *vajrasana*, my whole body is filled with bliss as I directly touch the Buddha. He lives today as he did in the past; his timeless realisation has not dwindled one bit even though since then many civilisations have risen and fallen. His full potential is just as real and his path just as clear.

When coming to Bodh Gaya I expected to come away with a deeper understanding and experience of the Buddha. I have that, but also when I am here I am delighted to connect with a deeper understanding and experience of Sangha, like a secret unexpected jewel of delight. Each and every one is their own unique person, moving around the tree in a flow of movement or just sitting in stillness, like a field of merit and influence protecting the Buddha and expressing his nature. If my mind strays into pride and arrogance towards any of my brothers and sisters, I silently repeat these verses: 'I am not superior to you' ... ''I am not inferior to you' ... 'I am not the same as you'. It helps me to maintain the spirit.

It doesn't matter what clothes a person wears. We cannot say who is a genuine practitioner just by the cloth on their body. The practices and intentions come from deep within the human heart, and the human heart is a mystery of such complexity and depth that it is impossible for one person to judge another. We may get a glimpse or a hint but we cannot know them completely or judge what their motives truly are.

In other places we are struggling against the stream of samsara, outside us and within us, in an effort to take refuge. But here everything is taking refuge. There is a collective and historical accumulation of merit in that direction, we just need to come here, plunge in, and let go into the stream. Being together here helps us to do this, helps us let go of our attachment to tribes and groups. Bodh Gaya makes us relate to each other on the deepest principle: the Buddha's realisation.

The Buddha's unconditional nature is always here as a possibility if we can only wake up from that dream we call our 'self'.

Unfold, secret symbol of the heart! Come forth with rains of meaning, and engulf my being with profound insight. Turn my views of 'self' on their heads. Your way is the deepest spring, infinitely more nourishing than the shallow pool of 'self'. Let me drink deep from the pure original source of mind, that comes untouched, untainted, pure and stainless from the deepest well. Hidden symbol, hidden mind, come forth in colour, touch or smell, or dream, whatever form, sound or feeling gives the slightest clue or sign. Present yourself to me. Shatter the 'I' in which 'I' hide, break free my samsaric grip and let *sunyata* be my only refuge. No refuge, no self, no Buddha, no path, no Nirvana, no samsara, nowhere to come from, nowhere to go ...

Bodh Gaya can leave a powerful karmic imprint on your psyche. In the face of fear and at the point of death there is some weight of connection to the Buddha's Enlightenment. Every person should come here, for it is here that the world's most significant event happened.

It is easy to imagine Bodh Gaya as an accumulation of merit that has built up from devotion and practice over centuries. There is also the accumulation of practice that we all create together. Each one of us who connects in some way with the Buddha is part of the rich fabric of Bodh Gaya, and each time we come here we help create this great place. Each one of us working away, using our own practices, we soften for ourselves and each other that hard distinction between self and other. We dissolve the distinction between the Buddha's mind and our own; each moment we serve the Buddha and make an effort through our imagination, his qualities drip drip into us. His presence as a teacher is just as ready to touch us as it was 2,600 years ago. If we open our hearts, maybe just a drop of his beauty can drop into them, followed by another drop, and yet another, until these drops become a flowing stream and a mighty ocean.

🍃

Bodhitree Mike said: 'Merit is an accumulation and repetition of virtuous action; it is a momentum, so here your merit is increased because of the blessing power of this place.'

🍃

Pilgrims making quiet solitary prayers from deep within: no statues, no fuss, just simple-hearted people delighted to meet the Buddha.

🍃

In amongst the blur of colour is the flash of a white kesa and a blue shirt.

🍃

One morning on the way to breakfast I met a Thai princess having an open session at her temple, and after that I found a dead dog lying on the ground. Bodh Gaya truly is a place of extremes, from the sublime to the disgusting.

🍃

Walking on the earth where the Buddha walked, touching his energy with my bare feet, feeling his profound knowledge, I soak up his peace.

♩

Silent prayers welling up deep from within, verses of beauty, reverence and aspiration.

Silent prayers, the secret depths of the human heart offering itself in service.

Silent prayers, profound gratitude for the Buddha's efforts to wake up from his mortal sleep.

Silent prayers, love, joy and aspiration verses, silently reciting verses to inspire a glimmer of the Buddha's full potential in our hearts and minds.

♩

Bodh Gaya is a symphony of practice. Music that is not heard is still music, but listening and witnessing each other is a more collective and deeper way. Bodh Gaya gives us a chance to reflect on what that means.

♩

One day at the temple I walked in the footsteps of a man singing a Japanese song, a divine devotional song, describing the indescribable, expressing the inexpressible, resonating with profound truth and beauty, reaching beyond all words I know. His gift was profound, and I drank it in like a man on the point of dying of thirst. In his deep devotion, he circled the temple time and time again. Although he was moving through the crowd, his voice cut through all the mantras and the noise like a sharp sword cuts easily through silk, calling out the way to the deepest mystery. I have felt such transcending beauty through sound on only two other occasions in my life: listening to Pachelbel's canon at the Academy of Ancient Music, and hearing Zakir Hussain playing the tabla at a live performance. Like all things, the Japanese singer went on his way, and I was left only with the memory and the feeling. He illuminated me to some degree, although we didn't talk; we probably don't even speak the same language. This is the power of Bodh Gaya. Here as a Sangha we help each other to wake up bit by bit, and remind each other of the goal. I am proud he is my brother in the Dhamma.

19

A full moon night
at the temple

We did not reach our destination until after midnight and found
the place completely deserted. Even the roadside boutiques
were closed and a profound silence reigned. As we neared the
Maha Bodhi Temple, the central tower of which was silhouetted
against the starry sky, to our astonishment we saw that in
every niche of the great building, as well as on the numerous
votive stupas by which it was surrounded, a little oil lamp was
burning. There must have been thousands of lamps. So tranquil
was the scene that it was not difficult to believe they had been
placed there in worship of the Buddha not by any human agency
but by the invisible hands of devas.

Sangharakshita describes arriving at Bodh Gaya
at night (*Moving against the Stream*)

At the community we prepare for a night at the temple. We
collect our gear and walk in a line like warriors prepared
for battle. With us we have mosquito nets, jumpers, snacks,
head torches, water and flowers. We meet other friends at
the temple, all ready for our great test of all-night practice.
At 9pm we enter, and the gates of the temple are sealed
shut. We cannot leave until 4am, when the temple will
open again. We are sealed in like a furnace.

We settle into our position near the bodhi tree and
start with a puja, then do some meditation. At night at
the temple there is a much more reflective, peaceful and
retreat-like quality. Apart from the cries of night birds,

an occasional dog barking and the ongoing whine of mosquitoes, it is silent. There are people present, but no one is talking. People are here to practise.

I walk all around the different parts of the temple and there is absolute silence. I enjoy sitting for a while by the Muchalinda Lake, then spend time just sitting with the Buddha. Touching my head on his stone feet, I feel blessed.

Scattered all around the foot of the tree there are 20 or 30 mosquito nets with people sitting under them in meditation posture. By 1am snoring emerges from beneath some of them, as meditation gives way to sleep. Some other meditators without mosquito nets lie down now too, like fallen soldiers on a battlefield. I am reminded of my five year old son Archie, who fights to the bitter end even when he is extremely tired, until sleep finally takes over.

The full moon pierces our temple and saturates it in a golden hue. Pure and tranquil, it stirs my heart. Four beautiful aspects of my life conspire, like a four-way eclipse: it is full moon, we are at the bodhi tree, it is night time and it is silent. The feeling is dreamlike. By 1.30am some of our own Triratna soldiers have fallen asleep and joined in with the snoring. Buddhavajra is by far the winner of the loudest snorer contest.

One tiny woman walks around and around with the speed and determination of someone who knows what she wants, like a woman entering a shop on a big sale day just as it opens. Another woman stretches forwards from her sitting position. I assume she is stretching her back from lots of meditation, but she is still like that after two hours, so she must have succumbed to sleep.

At 4am the gate is opened and the morning shift arrives. Mantras break the spell of silence, the early practitioners add a burst of new life and energy, and the temple continues its flow of day and night ongoing practice. Leaving, we sit and have chai at the temple gates, discussing our various night experiences. During the evening I collected three bodhi leaves – a good number, as it is hard to get them during the daytime.

20

Beating the drum
of the Dhamma

In a world that has become blind
I go to beat the drum of the Deathless.
                    From the *Ariyapariyesana Sutta*

When I asked Sangharakshita what spirit we should aim to create at our centre, he said: 'I call it the spirit of beating the drum of the Dhamma; we should not forget the Dhamma.' That sparked my imagination. The drum of the Dhamma pounds away ignorance. Every drum-beat, every ounce of energy, beats out the truth. Every confused state of mind fears to hear its boom, the thunderous sound of reality through which all beings are freed. The drum is like a heartbeat beating out the Buddha's Dhamma through countless millennia. World systems and galaxies throughout time and space have followed this primal rhythm, and we can hear it too, the beat of an eternal drum striking directly into our being. It strikes at the heart of woe and shatters the heart of darkness, breaking the fetters that bind and leaving us to resonate with it in full liberated awareness. When we hear the drum, we must respond and allow its timeless communication to speak to us.

In the temple at night I am reminded of my original inspiration to come here and serve when I arrived here in 1998. It made me feel that I wanted to help others to experience the same faith that arose in me. That vision is still the same today. All that matters to me in the face of suffering and death is what I can give to others and the qualities I have deep in my heart. Nothing else matters. Money doesn't matter, status doesn't matter, beautiful objects don't matter.

My spiritual focus is on two fronts. Firstly, I need to deepen my practice so that I can develop the qualities needed to fall apart, experience humiliation and loss of functioning and die, and not be overwhelmed by grief, sadness and fear. This is easier said than done, as to do it I need to make a massive shift in my 'self'-identity, which I find very hard to let go of because I am very attached to who I think I am. I need to focus on all of the traditional practices that align my expectations to be in line with reality so I am not disappointed or turned upside down by what happens. And when I am challenged and turned upside down, I must use that opportunity to deepen my understanding of the way things are rather than becoming frustrated and angry. Secondly, I need to leave something for others, a kind of legacy from which others can benefit long after I've gone. I want to create situations that have a life and momentum beyond me, so they will carry on when I can't contribute to them any more. My work at the centre in Bodh Gaya is part of that legacy.

No one person has the power to make this happen, but we can live and work together, inspired by the life and liberation of the Buddha. Every single person here plays a part in shaping the future of Buddhism. Every single act of faith and devotion, every single prostration, every single prayer, shapes people's hearts and minds and therefore shapes the spirit and intention of this place, which in turn shapes Buddhism and humanity as a whole.

It is individual practitioners, whatever their tradition, who transform their hearts and minds and collectively create the beauty of this place. It is here under the bodhi tree that we are constantly reminded that the Buddha's realisation is achievable by us. The path has been laid down and all traditions know its steps, and where it leads.

The Buddha struggled in the same way we do with life and its ups and downs and with suffering. All men and woman are capable of realising what he realised, breaking the powerful bonds that bind us to the cycles of suffering in birth and death. The Buddha is an example; he has shown us the way. It is up to us to make the effort to wake up as he did.

One flame has been lighting another for thousands of years, ever since the time of the Buddha, and we are now the guardians of that flame. Let us not fail in our duty of care. Bodh Gaya is a world in itself, populated by people from many places on earth. If we can live and practise in harmony, we can be an example to the followers of other world religions, and strengthen the role of Buddhism in the world. The focus on the Dhamma here through countless traditions all focused around the great bodhi tree can reach out across the world and through many generations.

Every single pilgrim and practitioner, as well as each of the Dhamma followers of many traditions who live here permanently, helps to shape Bodh Gaya's future. We are not just passive observers. Whatever our input, large or small, we are adding to Bodh Gaya's fabric and collective consciousness. We are part of the ongoing puja and practice that is the Mahabodhi temple. Everyone brings their own piece of life to this place, their own flavour of practice. So Bodh Gaya is a place of great sharing and exchanging of who we are both individually and as traditions. Here we both give and receive. When freedom was won at this very spot, there was a fundamental shift, the opening of a new doorway of human potential. No longer need we be victims to greed, hatred and confusion. We have entered a new era of possibilities.